CANDICE OLSON
BEDROOMS

PHOTOGRAPHS BY BRANDON BARRÉ

WILEY

John Wiley & Sons, Inc.

Library of Congress Control Number: 2012937950

ISBN: 978-1-118-27681-5 (pbk)
ISBN: 978-1-118-29539-7; 978-1-118-29540-3; 978-1-118-29541-0 (ebk)

Printed in the United States of America

10 9 8 7 6 5 4 3 2 1

Book production by John Wiley & Sons, Inc., Composition Services

Note to the Readers:
Due to differing conditions, tools and the individual skills, John Wiley & Sons, Inc. assumes no responsibility for any damages, injuries suffered, or losses incurred as a result of following the information published in this book. Before beginning any project, review the instructions carefully, and if any doubts or questions remain, consult local experts or authorities. Because codes and regulations vary greatly, you always should check with authorities to ensure that your project complies with all applicable local codes and regulations. Always read and observe all of the safety precautions provided by manufacturers of any tools, equipment, or supplies, and follow all accepted safety procedures.

Book design by Tai Blanche
Cover design by Susan Olinsky

Updates to this book are available on the Downloads tab at this site: http://www.wiley.com/Wiley/CDA/WileyTitle/productCd-118276817.html. If a Downloads tab does not appear at this link, there are no updates at this time.

To my husband Jurij,

who knows the cure for chilly feet

under the covers is a warm heart

and a good spooning!

**C**andice Olson is one of North America's leading designers and most recognized media personalities. As designer and host of *Divine Design with Candice Olson* and *Candice Tells All,* she is a favorite with viewers on W Network in Canada and HGTV in the U.S. Each week she brings a wealth of design experience and an attitude that is smart, witty, and truly unique into over 115 million North American households.

After earning her degree from the School of Interior Design at Ryerson University in Toronto, Candice launched an exciting commercial and residential design business. Considered "the one to watch" by *The New York Times,* Candice continued to receive accolades and media attention for her distinctive and exceptional work.

Candice's foray into television began when a local TV station profiled one of her award-winning design projects. Her unique approach to residential design and engaging personality led to a weekly stint as a design contributor to the show. Viewer demand for "more Candice!" led to the creation of the hit series, *Divine Design with Candice Olson.* Candice and the show quickly won a huge and loyal audience and went on to achieve a milestone of over 200 episodes after eight seasons. *Divine Design with Candice Olson* continues to receive rave reviews and recognition around the world, including the more than 160 countries where the series has aired.

In 2005, Candice launched "The Candice Olson Collection," her own successful brand of licensed product lines, including upholstered furniture, fabrics, wallpaper, lighting, carpeting, case goods, and bedding. Candice's signature style is one she describes as "a fusion of traditional form, scale, and proportions, with the clean, crisp, simple beauty of modern design." For more information, visit www.candiceolson.com.

The continued demand for "more Candice!" brought her to wider audiences through guest appearances on television shows such as *The Today Show, Regis and Kelly, The View,* and *The Oprah Winfrey Show.* Candice writes a bi-weekly newspaper column syndicated in over 400 newspapers across North America and is a frequent contributor to design magazines both in Canada and the U.S. For two seasons, Candice has been featured as a Celebrity Judge for the prime time hit reality show, *HGTV Design Star.*

Candice spends her free time with her family, skiing in the winter and relaxing at the beach in summer. A native of Calgary, Alberta, she lives in Toronto with her husband and two children.

WANT TO KNOW WHERE CANDICE SHOPS?

As her fans around the world know, Candice Olson sources out the most amazing products from her favorite suppliers across North America, and now you can gain access too!

Visit **www.candiceolsonbooks.com** to find detailed information about the materials and products from all of her spectacular rooms in this book.

Happy shopping!

Table of Contents

Master Bedrooms

2 Personal Spaces

3

Rooms for Kids

INTRODUCTION

imply by nature, the bedroom is one of the most intimate and personal rooms in the home. And where you are in your personal life at any given point in time certainly helps influence its design.

In earlier years, my bedroom was about personal self-expression. Out of both interest and financial necessity, a favorite band or movie poster became wall art. I cobbled together an eclectic mix of brightly patterned bargain basement linens, a DIY headboard made from vinyl-wrapped acoustical tiles, and a ceiling painted in shades of high-gloss silver. The look was bold and edgy and reflected the urban lifestyle of a young working woman.

When I met my husband, my bedroom took a decidedly romantic turn. Candles and soft lighting, reflective mirror and crystal, layers of lush textures, patterns, and rich colors set the mood. With two people sharing a space, more practical considerations, such as clothing storage, dressing, and grooming, came into play in our tiny downtown house.

Then, with the birth of our children (often a by-product of romantic bedrooms!), I have to be honest: Design was not at the forefront of our concerns when we saw our bedroom taken over by baby basinets, wipes, and monitors! Once the post-partum dust settled, our bedroom became simply our bunker—a room to escape to for a few hours of shut-eye while our children discovered sleeping through the night was something they might like to entertain on a more permanent basis!

Now with bigger kids and a slightly larger home, our needs have once again shifted. My electronic calendar is a blur of color-coded activities as our days overflow with the frenetic pace of two busy careers and two kids involved in everything under the artistic or athletic sun. Our bedroom is now our sanctuary, a place where we decompress, debrief, and reconnect at the end of a long, busy day. Its design reflects

the antithesis of what our lives are all about. Where our days are chaotic, our bedroom reflects calm with simple, clean lines; quiet, low-contrast color; and muted patterns. Both my husband and I are in the design and building business, constantly surrounded by people and having to juggle schedules, tradesmen, and craftsmen. Our bedroom, however, is totally private. I'll admit a king size bed makes it easier for Sunday morning family snuggles, but for the most part, it is a room of solace and peace, and the style and function of the space are conducive to just that.

No matter what the time or personal stage of your life, successful bedroom design affords equal parts physical and visual comfort. Design choices made about color and pattern or even the most elaborate lighting schemes take a back seat when night falls and the senses are simultaneously simplified and amplified. Soft feels so much softer, silk is rendered silkier, when texture is the only experience. In no other room in the home is this balance of tactile and visual more important—and for a designer, more exciting—to create. The perfect combination makes the waking hours spent in the bedroom as dreamy as the slumber they eventually fade into.

1 MASTER BEDROOMS

FROM CAVERNOUS TO COZY

CHALLENGE

Michelle, a golf pro, and Bryan, a physical education teacher and former NCAA volleyball coach, had redecorated the rest of their new suburban home in a contemporary/traditional style, but when they got to the master bedroom, they had to call time out. It was huge—almost big enough for a volleyball court!—and very red. Yet with all that space, the closet was too small for the couple to share. The king-size bed was new, bought in an attempt to fill a large, dark alcove, but the rest of the furniture had been with Michelle since she was a teen. Clearly it was time for a new game plan.

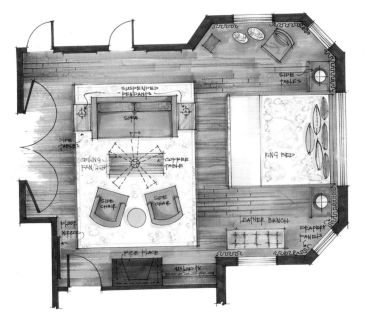

BEFORE: Michelle and Bryan's bedroom was very red and big enough to host a volleyball tournament. Even buying a king-size bed and floating a seating group in the bay window area couldn't make it seem less cavernous.

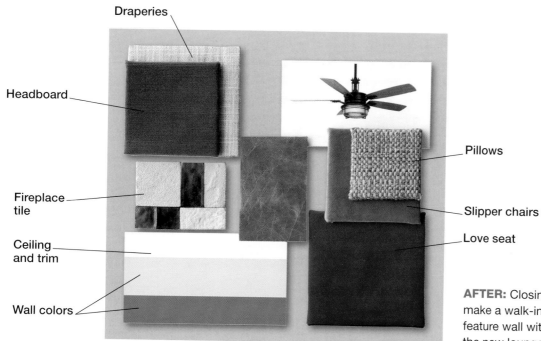

Draperies

Headboard

Pillows

Fireplace tile

Slipper chairs

Ceiling and trim

Love seat

Wall colors

AFTER: Closing off the bed alcove to make a walk-in closet provided a new feature wall with a fireplace that anchors the new lounge area. The window bay becomes a luxurious sleeping zone.

SOLUTION

- The first step was to reconfigure the whole space to make it function better. Since the couple needed better storage and had an abundance of floor space, I decided to close off the alcove where the bed had been and turn it into a roomy walk-in closet.

- The wall enclosing the new closet then became a fabulous feature wall for a new lounge area. I installed a beautiful new gas fireplace with a TV and media cabinet beside it. Comfy slipper chairs and a love seat turn this area into an intimate living room where the couple can relax after a long day or enjoy watching TV with their two boys.

- I moved the bed to the window bay and centered it under the largest window. Then I designed an upholstered headboard that would fit just below the sill. Because the couple's bed is a platform style, the headboard mounts on the wall instead of the bed frame.

- Instead of floor or table lamps beside the love seat, I opted for two pendant fixtures—every bedroom needs a couple of pendants! They create a wonderful feeling of intimacy. We couldn't get into the attic to install recessed lights, so I used monopoint lights around the perimeter of the room to wash light over the walls. Table lamps beside the bed allow for bedtime reading.

- A ceiling fan will help circulate cool air in summer and warm air in winter.

OPPOSITE: A cozy gas fireplace framed by gorgeous glass and natural stone tile makes a stunning focal point for the lounge area. We framed the fireplace wall with wood painted to match the adjacent walls, both to better showcase the tile and to eliminate the need to work it around the corner.

BELOW: Installing the flat-screen TV beside the fireplace lets Michelle and Bryan enjoy the TV and the fireplace at the same time. When the television is turned off, the black screen and frame blend in with the dark cabinetry below and virtually disappear.

STYLE ELEMENTS

- For the fireplace wall, I found a gorgeous glass and natural stone mosaic tile in shades of amber, caramel, and cognac. The combination of contemporary glass and traditional stone produces a timeless look, and the tile provided the jumping-off point for fabrics and paint—rich, yummy butterscotch for the feature wall and two plush slipper chairs, warm taupey cream for the remaining walls and draperies. For spicy contrast, I upholstered the love seat in rusty red and added a pair of lumbar pillows covered in caramel tweed.

- Michelle and Bryan love the light that pours in through five big windows, but when you're trying to sleep late, light isn't so good. To provide an efficient room-darkening system, I installed Roman blinds with blackout lining in each window. Linen drapery panels backed with dim-out lining also help with light control and make a luxurious backdrop for the bed.

- To pick up on the traditional style elsewhere in the house, I chose a ceiling fan with an oil-rubbed bronze finish, dark wood blades, and an amber light. The pendants have the same oil-rubbed finish and simple, classic shape, with amber-color shades.

- Low slipper chairs won't block the view of the TV from anywhere in the room. I had them upholstered with skirts to avoid having too many skinny legs in the seating group. For the love seat, I chose a model with low arms because it offers lots of area for seating.

- Side tables with mirrored tops blend traditional and contemporary styles and will reflect the light of the pendants above them (see page 23).

RIGHT: Layers of luxurious fabrics dress the bed in color, texture, and elegant pattern, and floor-to-ceiling drapery panels soften the windows. To unify all five windows, I used drapery rods with elbow ends that allow you to connect rods along angled walls. Roman shades with blackout lining provide light control for those late mornings in bed. (What late mornings? Michelle and Bryan have two small boys!)

RIGHT: Pendant lamps take the place of table or floor lamps beside the love seat. Nailhead trim along the low arms of the love seat adds a little sparkle.

BELOW: As on the love seat, nailhead trim outlines the headboard, a nice bit of repetition that helps tie the room together. Layers of pillows in touchable textures add warmth and color to the space.

A ROYAL MARRIAGE

CHALLENGE

Simon is a dyed-in-the-wool Anglophile who loves all things British. His ideal bedroom would be in the English medieval style, with a moat and drawbridge thrown in for good measure. Kristine, on the other hand, leans toward a lighter, more modern look that's warm and luxurious. Both of them agreed that their dark, dated master bedroom needs help, and that's where I come in. Wearing my marriage counselor hat *and* my designer hat, I'll breathe some fresh air into formal, traditional English style and create a room that pleases them both.

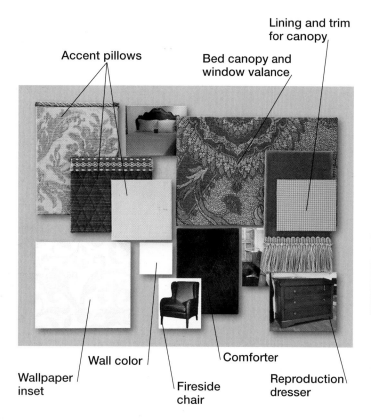

Lining and trim for canopy

Accent pillows

Bed canopy and window valance

Wallpaper inset

Wall color

Fireside chair

Comforter

Reproduction dresser

BEFORE: This dark, dated bedroom was as far from Simon's dreams of Jolly Old England as it was from Kristine's vision of a warm, modern, luxurious retreat.

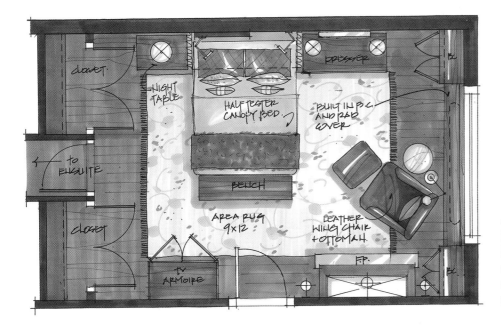

AFTER: There's no moat or drawbridge, but with a carved, luxuriously canopied bed, regal fabrics, and reproduction antique bedside chests, this bedroom definitely speaks with a royal British accent!

SOLUTION

- I start by adding architectural interest. Crown moldings, panel moldings, and a handsome new fireplace give the room the right "bones" for an English country house look.

- Installing the fireplace required pulling a gas line into the house and running a flue through the roof, and the results are practical as well as aesthetic. The gas insert keeps the room toasty in winter, and the faux coal firebox (instead of logs) says "merrie olde England." The prefab hearth and surround add traditional character without the cost of custom.

- To provide plenty of storage for the couple's library as well as clothing, I designed a pair of bookshelves flanking the windows, with closed storage below. Linked by a custom-built radiator box, the units appear built-in and enhance the architectural character of the room.

- As the focal point of the room, the bed needed a regal presence. I designed a ceiling-mounted canopy with luxurious floor-to-ceiling curtains that not only frame the bed but also hide a chimney flue that runs up from the floor below. The canopy box is secured to the ceiling, and the draperies are mounted on tension rods inside the box. The valance attaches to the edges of the box with hook-and-loop tape.

- For the light, bright feeling Kristine wanted, I painted the walls with two coats of warm antique white. Then I applied a shimmery, embossed damask wallpaper inside the panel-molding frames to add subtle sparkle, texture, and pattern to the walls.

OPPOSITE: Ahh, a cozy spot for King Simon (or Queen Kristine) to read by the fire! A gas-fueled, faux coal fireplace turns this corner of the bedroom into a focal point. Note how panel moldings divide the walls into picture-frame spaces. This is an easy way to add architectural character and depth to plain walls.

RIGHT: Moldings frame panels of iridescent, embossed damask wallpaper to add subtle shimmer and pattern to the walls. Sconces with a dark bronze finish cast an intimate glow.

RIGHT: Custom bookshelves linked by a radiator box bring loads of function to what had been an underutilized wall. With wooden shutters providing light control and privacy, all these windows needed was a beautiful pleated valance to tie them together.

ABOVE: Sumptuous silk-lined chenille draperies enclose the beautiful carved-wood bed. Mirrors glued into the panels on the closet doors serve as dressing mirrors and help expand the sense of space in the room.

STYLE ELEMENTS

- Gorgeous, rich fabrics play a key role in creating the English manor look Simon wanted. Working with a palette of rich reds, elegant greens, and soft taupes, I chose a chenille jacquard for the window valance, bed canopy, and draperies, with silk gingham for the lining. A quilted red chenille damask coverlet and velvet-trimmed throw pillows dress the bed in royal style. I even made up some pillows decorated with Simon's "family crest"!

- Kristine and Simon's old furniture was left over from their university days, so I replaced it with new pieces inspired by traditional English designs. Mismatched bedside chests, an entertainment-center armoire, and a leather-upholstered armchair and ottoman all draw on furniture styles from the seventeenth to the nineteenth centuries, creating that added-over-time look you'd find in the ancestral family manse.

- For lighting, I chose a clear glass lantern with simple lines to hang over the bed so it won't distract from the canopy. Sconces at the fireplace provide intimate lighting. Mismatched table lamps illuminate each side of the bed, and recessed fixtures around the perimeter of the room wash the walls with ambient light.

- Every bedroom needs a dressing mirror, so I put the closet doors to work with mirrors glued onto the door panels. The mirrored doors also reflect light and enlarge the illusion of space.

RIGHT: I chose a very simple glass lantern for the ceiling fixture to avoid competing with the bed canopy. Three candlestick lights evoke the Old World look Simon longed for.

BELOW: Bun feet, batwing drawer pulls, and a burled-wood finish highlight the eighteenth-century inspiration for this modern chest of drawers. It makes a great bedside table, with a pull-out shelf to hold bedtime reading and other necessities.

ABOVE: Pillows in a mix of velvets, chenilles, and satiny cottons help focus attention on the bed. I deliberately chose unmatched lamps for each side of the bed, but using black shades ties the two styles together.

REVVED-UP NEUTRALS

CHALLENGE

David and Nuala thrive on wilderness adventure, but when they decided to tackle the adventure of home remodeling and construction, well, they sort of met their match. Besides gutting the entire 1926 house, they had added a new master bedroom, and eight months into reconstruction, it was still unfinished and they were overwhelmed. Although they're thrill-seekers in the great outdoors, the couple played it so safe when it came to decorating decisions that they risked falling into boring and bland. My challenge was to bring a little excitement to the cool white tones they love and give them a bedroom that combines quiet elegance with a nod to nature.

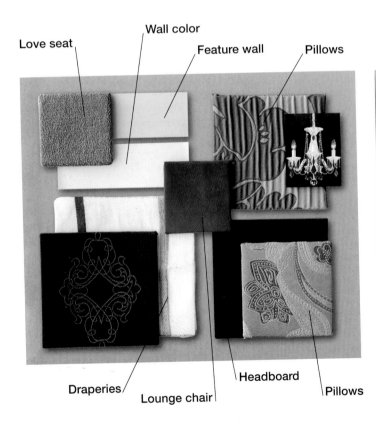

Love seat | Wall color | Feature wall | Pillows

Draperies | Lounge chair | Headboard | Pillows

BEFORE: With only the bones in place for the master suite addition, Nuala and David were in a quandary about finishing it in a way that reflected their personalities.

AFTER: Contrasting textures, a hint of large-scale pattern, and a range of dark and light tones add up to one very exciting neutral scheme! Earthy, natural tones balance the cool, contemporary grays for a look that's both rustic and refined.

SOLUTION

- Designed as a master suite, the addition already had a large walk-in closet in the bedroom area and a decorative fireplace in the section intended for a sitting room. A vaulted ceiling with skylights and a wall of windows made the bedroom end feel light and airy. Vintage windows and an old-fashioned radiator added a sense of history.

- Color is the key here: David and Nuala are most comfortable with white, so to rev that up a bit, I chose a range of dark and light grays for fabrics and wall color. I painted one wall a darker, cool blue-gray to make it a feature and a striking backdrop for the fireplace and bed. That's a bit adventurous!

- I chose creamy white for all of the woodwork, cabinetry, and ceilings. To ground the neutrals, I installed hardwood floors in a dark finish.

- Because the seating area is the first thing you see when you enter, I decided to make the nonfunctional fireplace a super-cool focal point that brings a little of the outdoors inside. We built a shallow box to fill the space between the mantel and the ceiling and packed it with tightly stacked pieces of hand-hewn logs.

- New floor-to-ceiling cabinetry with traditional crown moldings conceals the radiator and provides open and closed storage for the sitting area.

- A comfy new sofa centered on the fireplace gives David and Nuala a place to relax and read in front of the fireplace.

- A new upholstered headboard for the queen-size bed anchors the bedroom area.

- The vaulted ceiling was a major architectural feature, so I added a ceiling fan to draw attention to it and improve air flow year-round.

- Near the windows, there's space for a comfy, extra-wide chair, a console table, and a floor lamp for reading.

ABOVE: The ceiling fan calls attention to the lovely vaulted ceiling in the bedroom end of the suite. The rattan blades reinforce the theme of natural textures in the wooden blinds and the stacked-wood installation over the fireplace, and the brown color relates to the browns of flooring, furniture, and drapery fabric.

STYLE ELEMENTS

- Fabrics play off of the cool gray wall color, with a deep, rich charcoal-gray velvet for the headboard, blue-gray leather for an end-of-bed upholstered bench, and soft blue-gray for the sitting-room love seat. The striped linen drapery fabric brings together all of the colors in the room—white, blue-gray, and the brown of the floors and wooden tables.

- Contrasting textures liven things up in a neutral room, so I juxtaposed rustic with refined throughout the space. Crystal sconces are a sparkly surprise mounted on the firewood installation over the fireplace; shiny mirror-clad bedside chests and accent tables contrast with the soft, matte finish of velvet and suedelike microfiber fabrics.

- Woven wood blinds and rattan ceiling fan blades carry the natural texture of the firewood installation into the bedroom area, and the rattan suggests a hint of the exotic.

- To bring in eclectic touches that reflect David and Nuala's world travels, I chose a console table and a pair of vintage-look painted side chairs with Chinese-inspired lines, a faux zebra rug, and a variety of accessories from Africa and Asia.

OPPOSITE: The fireplace was never intended to be more than decorative, so I made sure it deserved the attention! This one-of-a-kind over-mantel installation consists of 5-inch-long pieces of hand-hewn logs glued into the custom-built box frame. I love the contrast of shiny mirror and sparkly sconces against the rough wood.

ABOVE: The new custom-built cabinet conceals the radiator in classic style. A crystal chandelier and matching sconces add character and ambience in keeping with the vintage style of the house, while contemporary accent tables, love seat, and a funky lamp behind the love seat give the room a modern vibe.

BELOW: A spacious walk-in closet, a key ingredient for any successful marriage, fills the wall opposite the bed. In addition to real natural textures, such as woven wood blinds and rattan, I included decorative pieces inspired by nature—such as the little side table with metal legs that imitate bamboo.

ABOVE: Flowy linen drapery panels frame the beautiful view and soften the architecture. It's up to the wooden blinds to provide privacy and block light.

ELEVATION

A SPACE-TAMING TRANSFORMATION

CHALLENGE

When you have a tiny space, you want more, but when you have a lot of space you're faced with the dilemma of what to do with it all. That was the problem facing Cathy and David. After living in an apartment in Japan that was the size of a shoebox, they now have a 3,800-square-foot house, and the master bedroom is the biggest room. Their queen-size bed is fine for Cathy, but for 6-foot-tall David, it's really too small. He likes to watch TV in bed, but Cathy would be just as happy if it disappeared. She'd like to somehow turn this vast space into a cozy, comfortable, romantic room that they both enjoy being in.

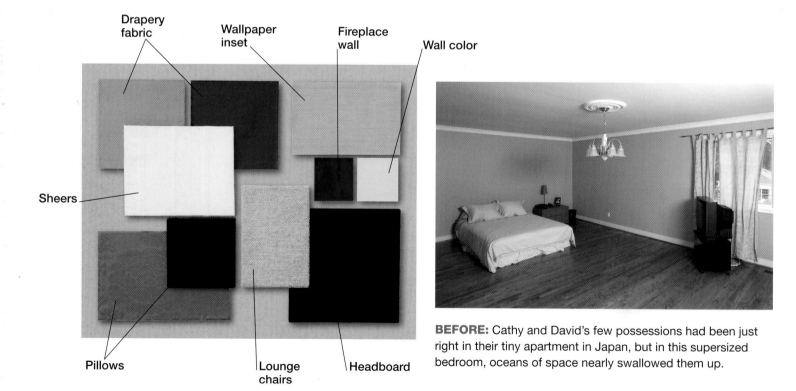

Drapery fabric · Wallpaper inset · Fireplace wall · Wall color · Sheers · Pillows · Lounge chairs · Headboard

BEFORE: Cathy and David's few possessions had been just right in their tiny apartment in Japan, but in this supersized bedroom, oceans of space nearly swallowed them up.

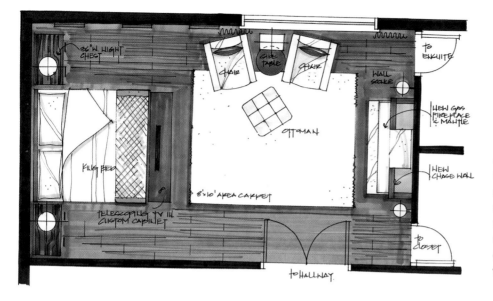

Labels in floor plan:
- 26"W NIGHT CHEST
- CHAIR
- SIDE TABLE
- CHAIR
- TO ENSUITE
- WALL SCONCE
- NEW GAS FIREPLACE & MANTLE
- OTTOMAN
- NEW CHASE WALL
- KING BED
- 8'x10' AREA CARPET
- TELESCOPING TV IN CUSTOM CABINET
- TO CLOSET
- TO HALLWAY

AFTER: Separating the room into sleeping and lounging zones takes advantage of the vast square footage and makes it functional. Dividing the walls into panels framed by moldings enriches the room with architectural character and tames the huge space with a feeling of order.

ABOVE: A new fireplace with a cast-stone surround creates a fabulous focal point that anchors the room. Dark bronze silk draperies edged with chocolate hang in vertical columns to make the long, squat window seem taller and to pick up on the repetition of the wall panels.

SOLUTION

- The first step to downsizing this enormous space was to break up the expanse of walls. I used molding to outline large panels and applied a shimmery gold strié wallpaper as insets. I then painted the walls and moldings a buttery cream color to contrast with the wallpaper. Now the walls aren't just big, they're big and beautiful!

- This room had plenty of square footage but only one window, and one entire end was taken up with traffic flow, with doors to the en suite bathroom and closet. I decided to create a focal point at this end by building out the wall between the two doors and installing a gas fireplace. The fireplace anchors a seating group that still leaves the traffic paths to the closet and bathroom free.

- The opposite end of the room became the sleeping zone. I positioned a supersize bed big enough for David to stretch out and still leave room for Cathy. Altering the widths of the panels on this wall frames the new headboard in the central module and makes it feel like part of the architecture.

- Finding just the right spot for David's TV was a little bit like Goldilocks and the Three Bears: above the fireplace was too far away, on one side of the bed or the other was awkward and too close. But at the end of the bed was just right, thanks to a state-of-the-art LCD television on a remote-controlled motorized lift. Tucked inside a cabinet that serves as the bed's footboard, the TV pops up when David wants to watch it and disappears when he doesn't. It can also swivel to face the lounge area. How cool!

LEFT: Installing the gas fireplace required building out the wall to accommodate flues and venting, but in this 23-foot-long room that was no problem! I chose a dramatically oversized fireplace surround to be in scale with the room. Its classic traditional style picks up on the crown molding that was already there.

STYLE ELEMENTS

- To create the cozy, romantic atmosphere Cathy wanted, I chose a yummy palette of lush, plush fabrics in bronze silk, chocolate velvet, cream chenille, and spicy red damask.

- I upholstered the tall headboard in chocolate velvet to anchor the sleeping zone and balanced it in the lounge zone with dark chocolate color on the wall framing the fireplace.

- A soft café-au-lait area rug anchors the seating area. Creamy chenille chairs can be positioned strategically for gazing at the fireplace or for watching TV, and a comfy espresso leather ottoman offers a place for Cathy and David to put their feet up.

- To disguise the squatty proportions of the room's only window, I dressed it with alternating columns of filmy sheers and bronze silk draperies. Edged with chocolate velvet, the silk columns pick up on the vertical divisions of the wall panels and have the same space-taming effect.

- New recessed lighting around the perimeter of the room makes the shimmery wallpaper panels glow. The old ceiling fixture was more appropriate for a dining room, so I replaced it with a traditional crystal pendant anchored by a dressy plaster-look medallion.

- David wanted a look that was a little contemporary with some traditional pieces mixed in, so I tucked a pair of Hepplewhite-style end tables beside the bed. The dark finish blends with the velvet headboard, while the lines contrast with the clean, contemporary look of the head and footboard.

the design

OPPOSITE: The fabrics in this room are a softer version of the architectural detailing that gives character to the space. Lush silks contrast with plush velvets, and a fiery damask adds a blaze of spicy color.

ABOVE: At the touch of a button, this super-cool television pops up out of a cabinet at the end of the bed, and it can also swivel to face the lounge area. Whoever controls the remote has the power!

A DREAMY RETREAT

CHALLENGE

Laura had survived a year of construction craziness renovating her 1940s bungalow and adding a second story when she met and married James. Now she was suffering from reno burnout, and the new second-story master bedroom still needed help. With soaring ceilings and lots of quirky angles, it was architecturally striking but difficult to furnish, and the high ceiling trapped warm air, making the room uncomfortably stuffy. There wasn't enough storage to accommodate James's clothes, which were scattered all over the house. With beige walls and beige carpet, the space was simply big, boring, and bland—a very long way from the romantic, restful retreat that both Laura and James dreamed of.

BEFORE: A soaring high ceiling and quirky angles had the potential to be interesting, but the beige walls, ceiling, and carpet translated into deadly dull and boring. The random furniture placement made the space feel temporary and uninviting.

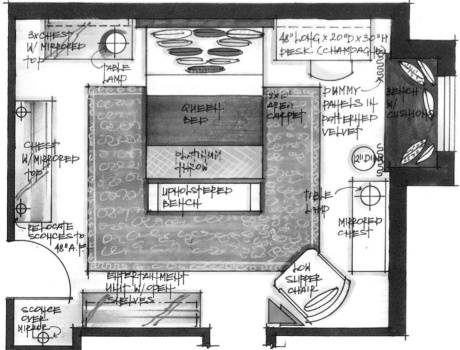

AFTER: A stunning Bombay-style fan and a beautiful, velvet-covered headboard turn the bed into an elegant focal point that transforms the whole mood of the room. Lighting turns the angles into an asset, and battens divide the soaring, angled walls, providing a logical place to start the blue wall color.

SOLUTION

- I started the whole process with the bed. With all the angles sending the eye in every direction, the room needed a focal point. I placed the bed front and center on the long wall and designed a sumptuous custom headboard to anchor it.

- Next, I addressed the air circulation issue with a "fan-tastic" solution above the bed: an awesome 11-foot-long motorized fan with six individual Bombay-style bamboo blades. Is six blades overkill? Not in this space! The scale of the fan and blades suits the sprawling scale of the room and makes a stunning showpiece that is also super-practical.

- Placement of junction boxes for lighting really wasn't optimal—there was one way high up on the ceiling and two more for sconces that didn't make sense in terms of function. I remedied the situation by running a T track system from the single source of electricity on the ceiling and installing pendant halogen track lights that spread the light around.

- One of the challenges with high, angled ceilings is where to stop the wall color and let the ceiling color take over. Installing 5-inch-wide flat battens about 10 feet above the floor divided "walls" from "ceiling" and unified all the angles. I then painted the walls below the battens with a soft blue to create a soothing, restful atmosphere.

- To solve the clothing storage problem, I brought in a ready-to-assemble dresser and three double-drawer units and gave them an upscale look with new crystal-clear cylinder handles and polished mirror tops. I bolted together the double-drawer units to make one long, low storage unit that doubles as a bedside table.

- James likes to watch TV in bed, and Laura sometimes needs to work on her laptop. I placed the TV on a low media stand on the wall opposite the bed and tucked a sleek console with drawers into the corner beside the bed for Laura. It can do triple duty—bedside table, office center, and vanity table.

RIGHT: The motorized fan system required installation of a reinforcement panel, which was painted to blend in with the walls. The blades will stir the air and help keep the second-story room comfortable. A settee upholstered in cocoa adds handy seating at the end of the bed.

OPPOSITE: A deep cushion and stacks of plush pillows turn the window seat into a romantic nook for snuggling. I loved the lattice-pattern velvet for the draperies so much, I used it for accent pillows and a gorgeous, silky-soft throw for the bed.

BELOW: A clean-lined Parsons table with two slim drawers can serve as office space or a vanity table for Laura. I paired it with a modern chair upholstered in crisp white.

STYLE ELEMENTS

- Delicious fabrics are key to giving this bedroom the premium, high-end look that Laura wanted. I upholstered the headboard with a crinkly, espresso-color crushed velvet that has the look of wood grain. Accent pillows in a beautiful beige paisley pick up on the beige wall-to-wall carpet and add creamy and platinum highlights to the scheme.

- To give the room's only window more presence and extend its apparent height, I topped it with a deep valance and framed it with floor-length draperies made of an incredibly sumptuous lattice-patterned velvet in a blue-toned charcoal. Velvet this silky and soft is too slippery to be sewn on a machine and must be stitched by hand, but it's worth the time and effort—it looks and feels fabulous.

- The window seat was just waiting to be "furnished," so I outfitted it with a plump box cushion covered in chocolate velvet and added layers of accent pillows to match those on the bed.

- I like to anchor the bed with an area rug to help define space. For this room I found a low-pile espresso-and-cream carpet with an absolutely perfect pattern to layer over the wall-to-wall broadloom carpet.

OPPOSITE: James's TV now sits on a handsome dark-wood entertainment unit that blends with the dressers. A single shelf above balances it with space for display.

RIGHT: This dresser came in a box, "some assembly required," and I took it one step further by replacing the hardware with crystal-clear, super-contemporary acrylic handles and a gleaming mirror top. Centering the dresser on this wall allowed me to use the junction boxes for sleek chrome sconces with crystal drops. For a dramatic contrast to the clean, modern lines of the dresser, I chose a flamboyant, ultra-baroque white mirror that screams "Look at me!"

OPPOSITE: Espresso crushed velvet upholsters the headboard and dresses two of the bed pillows. I picked up the color on the bed quilt and layered on pattern and texture with lattice-pattern velvet, paisley satin, and an elegant gray-and-white damask.

BELOW: Dramatic angles call for low furniture that can accommodate the architecture. An armless chair with a low, tufted back nestles into the corner beside a mirror-fronted dresser.

MODERN, MINIMALIST, AND MARVELOUS

CHALLENGE

Marcia and Frankie and their four children have a unique approach to decorating their home: They practice "design by democracy," giving everyone in the family (except the dog and the parrot) an equal voice in all decorating decisions. Unfortunately, because each person has firm opinions, they have a hard time finding consensus, and after two years the house was still in decorating limbo. Clearly it was time for an intervention! They agreed that the place to start was with the master bedroom, which was basically a blank slate, with bright purple walls, bare windows, and a bed.

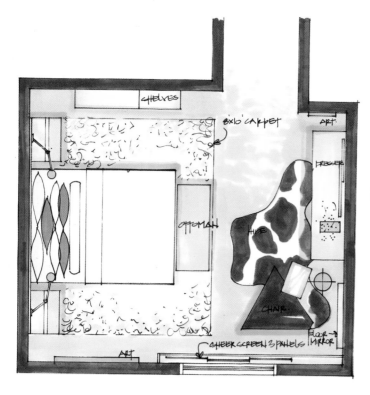

BEFORE: With bright purple walls and a lonely bed, the master bedroom was a blank slate rather than a restful retreat—clear evidence of design indecision.

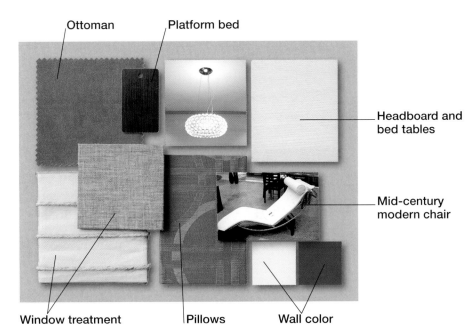

Ottoman   Platform bed

Headboard and bed tables

Mid-century modern chair

Window treatment   Pillows   Wall color

AFTER: A spectacular floating headboard and side tables with shelves make an ultra-modern statement in Frankie and Marcia's new bedroom. The bed's deep platform features drawers on one side.

ABOVE: Frankie and Marcia wanted a quiet retreat where he could read and she could relax at the end of the day, so I wrapped the room in the soothing neutrals that Marcia prefers and added bold pops of red to please Frankie's tastes. Espresso-brown wood tones, fabrics, and faux hide rug anchor the neutrals and balance the power of the red.

SOLUTION

- Frankie loves color and Marcia loves neutrals, but they both love minimalism, so I began by designing custom furniture to define the modern vibe. For the focal point: a new platform bed resting on a wood base with drawers for storage. For the "wow" factor: a fabulous headboard composed of three deep panels, two of tight-grain ash sandwiching an engineered product made from compressed reed and grass. Floating tables with shelves and built-in sconces flank the bed, and a long cabinet appears suspended on the opposite wall.

- To cover the windows, I designed shoji-inspired sliding screens that run on a track and fall in wide panels from near the ceiling to the floor. Because they're so much taller and wider than the windows, they become a wall feature, like a tapestry or piece of art. I used an incredible organza with jute woven through it and backed it with neutral linen so the screens will block light when pulled across the windows. A wooden valance painted to match the wall hides the track and blends in with the architecture.

- When it came to choosing wall color, there was no need to vote—Marcia and Frankie both won! I painted three walls a light, neutral color I knew Marcia would love. The fourth wall, opposite the bed, became a feature with fiery red paint to please Frankie.

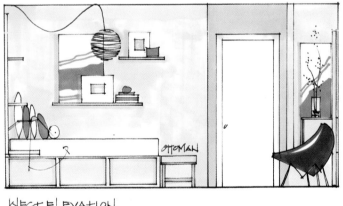

WEST ELEVATION
1/2" = 1'-0"

EAST ELEVATION
1/2" = 1'-0"

STYLE ELEMENTS

- In keeping with modernist style, the furniture lines emphasize the horizontal, with clean, rectangular shapes and smooth, flat cabinet faces. I used ash stained a natural tone for a light, fresh look, with dark wood for the base of the bed to anchor it visually.

- To bring Frankie's favorite red off the wall and into the room, I accented the bed with a pair of pillows covered in a gorgeous red fabric with a woven gold pattern. They play beautifully against the deep brown and crisp white pillows that Marcia likes.

- Puck lights on the bottom of the floating cabinet enhance the illusion of weightlessness. Over the bed, I hung a spectacular chandelier made of small acrylic balls that refract the light and bring some excitement into this cool minimalist space.

- Frankie loves modernism, so I gave him a classic mid-century modern-style chaise where he can read in comfort.

- At the end of the bed, a red ottoman serves as a coffee table or a handy catchall, with a shelf for stashing books underneath. A beautiful beige rug layered over the existing carpet adds some texture.

OPPOSITE: It's magic! The cabinet almost seems to levitate, thanks to the puck lights installed on the bottom to throw light on the walls and floor below. Marcia's TV is tucked into this unit so she can watch her favorite show—*Divine Design!*

BELOW: Three long panels of linen-backed organza hang from tracks hidden by the wooden valance. The panels slide back and stack over each other to expose the windows.

A ROOM OF THEIR OWN

CHALLENGE

Andrew and Christine had put off starting a family until their careers were established. Then they went from having one child to three in the course of just 18 months! Life was suddenly crazy, and their third-floor bedroom now held a crib and toys as well as their own bed and belongings. They're desperate for a quiet refuge they can retreat to at the end of the day, free of toys, bottles, and children. They're also worried about the exposed radiators, which can get super-hot and pose a hazard to unsuspecting little fingers.

BEFORE: Andrew and Christine had positioned their bed under the windows to block access to the radiators, but the arrangement didn't make the best use of the space. Old campaign-style dressers tucked under the eaves underscored the cramped feeling induced by steeply pitched ceilings.

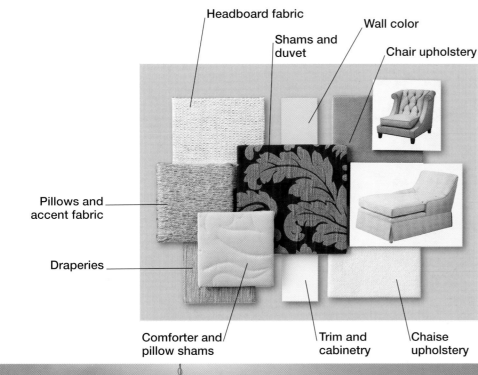

Headboard fabric

Shams and duvet

Wall color

Chair upholstery

Pillows and accent fabric

Draperies

Comforter and pillow shams

Trim and cabinetry

Chaise upholstery

AFTER: Blissfully free of baby clutter, the master bedroom is now an elegant, restful retreat. A long radiator box under the windows allows heat to escape but protects the children from a potential hazard. A new bank of built-in cabinetry masks the sloped ceiling and blends with the Mission style of the house.

SOLUTION

- The house was big enough for each child to have a bedroom, so I sent the crib and toys to the second floor and banished the old, campaign-style dressers.

- To take care of safety issues with the radiators, I designed some beautiful grill-front boxes to cover them and still allow the heat to escape.

- The oddly angled ceiling was part of the old house's charm, but it also presented a challenge for furniture placement. I nestled the bed on one long wall under the eaves and designed a bank of cabinetry to fit along the opposite wall. To keep it from looking like a big slab of storage, I designed the center section to project about 6 inches into the room. The television fits snugly into the top half, with drawers below for more storage.

- To give the bed more presence as the focal point of the room, I designed a sturdy upholstered headboard outlined with nailhead trim. An antique bench at the end of the bed serves as display space or a catchall—or a place for the kids to play when they're invited in!

- A quirky dormer was a little cramped but had just enough room for a luxurious chaise.

OPPOSITE: Wacky angles seem to disappear when walls and ceiling are painted the same platinum hue. I dressed the dormer window with a scaled-down version of the valance over the long wall of windows and reserved the draperies for the feature windows. Room-darkening woven wood blinds balance all the cool metallics with rustic texture.

STYLE ELEMENTS

- The radiator boxes and the new bank of storage pick up on the Mission-style detailing of the house and look like part of the architecture. I painted them to match the trim so they blend seamlessly into the room.

- Bedrooms are all about fabrics, and my choices here were geared toward creating the most soothing, sumptuous environment imaginable to pamper this hardworking, crazy-busy couple. In keeping with the home's traditional character, I selected conservative patterns such as damask, paisley, and chenille, but I gave them a modern twist with a palette of pewter, platinum, and silvery blue-gray. The headboard fabric is a soft linen with a glittery metallic thread that catches the light.

BELOW: Upholstered in soft blue-gray velvet, a pair of my "Piper" chairs offers old-fashioned elegance with button-tufted backs and rolled arms. The new storage cabinetry puts the TV where it can be seen easily without being a focal point in the room.

RIGHT: I had a greatly enlarged version of the damask pattern on the bed etched onto a sheet of mirror for the dormer wall. The mirror not only expands the sense of space and light, it also reflects unusual patterns on the chaise and window—how cool!

- The windows are all about function and beauty. A traditional flat valance hides the mechanics, and the draperies simply push back along the sides of the radiator box. I chose a shimmery silk that picks up on the pewter tones, and because silk and south-facing windows do not make good friends, I lined the draperies with blackout lining. Woven wood blinds add rustic natural texture to balance all the metallics and will darken the room for sleeping—when the kids are old enough to let Mom and Dad sleep in!

- To anchor the bed area, I layered a luscious wool-and-silk-blend rug over the existing carpet. The paisley design is another traditional reference, but I supersized it for a more updated look and kept the color contrast low for a whisper-quiet effect.

- I love the space-expanding qualities of mirrors, and for this room I didn't settle for any ordinary framed mirror. A custom mirror etched with a design inspired by the damask fabric is mounted (carefully) on the wall of the dormer, where it reflects light and casts spectacular shadows on the surrounding walls.

- Paint color is the last decision I make, after all the fabrics and finishes are chosen. To pull them all together, I coated the walls and ceiling with the same soft platinum hue, creating an envelope of restful color.

CHALET CHIC

CHALLENGE

Marriage is about compromise, and so is design. After a successful international career as a downhill skier, four-time Olympic competitor Brian has put aside his skis and embarked on a new life that includes a new wife, Heather, and will soon include twin girls. But his large third-floor bedroom hadn't yet made the transition to married life: Rustic and masculine, it lacked storage and lighting and looked like an outdated ski lodge. Heather's style is more urban, modern, and glam-fabulous—and she was tired of living out of boxes! My challenge: to strike a balance and create a bedroom that pleases them both.

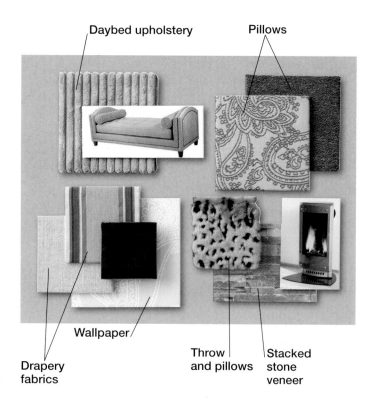

Daybed upholstery · Pillows · Wallpaper · Drapery fabrics · Throw and pillows · Stacked stone veneer

BEFORE: Brian's pine-and-plaid master bedroom made no concessions to his new bride's tastes—or to her stuff, which was stashed in boxes around the room.

AFTER: A little bit masculine, a little bit feminine, the new bedroom combines rustic textures with sophisticated pattern and gender-neutral color to create a perfectly balanced, warm and inviting master bedroom.

SOLUTION

- First comes function: I designed a full-blown closet system that will hold all of Heather's clothes and some of Brian's (see page 75). No more boxes! The custom cabinetry includes a dressing mirror *and* a mirrored cabinet for Heather's accessories, as well as a spot for Brian's TV.

- A new king-size bed with a luxurious, cocoon-like headboard anchors the sleeping area on one side of the room.

- At the other end of the room, under the steeply pitched roof, I nestled a daybed into the dormer (see page 76). This will be a little oasis for Heather where she can catch a quick nap—which she will need with twins!

- Brian was losing his home office to the nursery, so I tucked a rustic wooden farm table and office chair against the wall beside the dormer.

- Between the bedroom zone and the dormer, I created a restful lounge area. The focal point here is a stunning new feature wall of stacked stone and a petite free-standing gas fireplace. I built out the wall beside the old exposed brick to make room for the flue and gas lines and then clad the entire wall with stone veneer. The veneer is made from pieces of real stone that are glued together like tile. It's easy to apply with mortar and gives a fantastic rustic look at a fraction of the expense (and weight) of traditional stacked stone.

- Lighting is always key in my designs. Although I prefer recessed fixtures for beautiful, wall-washing illumination, I couldn't use them here because there was no room to work in the attic. Track lighting was the only option, and it's a good alternative—less expensive than recessed lights, easier to install, and easily directed to put light where you want it.

LEFT: The sleek, clean lines of this petite free-standing fireplace will appeal to Heather's design sensibilities, while the rugged stacked-stone veneer on the feature wall speaks to Brian's fondness for rustic style.

ABOVE: The headboard, a design called "Giselle," takes on a masculine look when covered in chocolate-brown leather. It evokes a men's club wing chair that enfolds you in cocoon-like comfort. Crisp white linens and faux leopard print pillows and throw give a nod to Heather's high-style, glam tastes. Paisley wallpaper is elegant and gender-neutral.

STYLE ELEMENTS

- Creating a his-and-hers space was mostly about balancing styles that were at opposite ends of the spectrum. I started with fabrics: durable buffalo leather upholstery for him, a faux leopard print for her (nothing says chic and sophisticated like a kitty cat!). A gender-neutral pear-green and bark-brown stripe for the draperies provided the jumping-off point for the room's color scheme and inspired the celery-green corded velvet for the daybed.

- After applying a rich cream color to the walls, I gave the wall behind the bed some extra glamour with a creamy paisley wallpaper. Paisley came from Persia and has been around forever. Here it adds a touch of high style without being too feminine, and its color blends perfectly with the stacked-stone wall.

- For the windows, I found wonderful bamboo and jute blinds that pick up on the green, brown, and cream color scheme. They bring in the woodsy character that Brian likes and will provide light control. Heather will appreciate the couture details in the draperies: the stripes are hidden inside the pleats at the top, giving a solid-green effect that's repeated in the deep, solid-green band at the bottom. In between, the pleats open out to reveal the brown-and-cream stripes.

- I painted the Shaker-style custom storage unit white to blend with the room's trim work, making it seem more like part of the architecture.

- Unmatched bedside tables balance a mirror-fronted cabinet for her with a dark wood nightstand for him. Matching über-cool bedside lamps pair natural twigs with frosted white acrylic in an ultra-chic contemporary design that's as much a sculpture as it is a lamp. I call it Chalet Chic!

OPPOSITE: An overstuffed armchair and ottoman upholstered in chocolatey buffalo leather offer comfy seating in front of the fireplace.

LEFT: A wall of new Shaker-style custom cabinetry fills what had been an empty, unfinished niche where Brian's clothes hung on a metal coat rack. The unit stores all of Heather's clothes and accessories and accommodates Brian's TV.

A fabulous daybed upholstered in plush corded velvet fits right into the dormer, creating a restful oasis for Heather. A gooseneck sconce with a shade gives her light for reading. The long pine table under the eaves is Brian's new home office.

IN PERFECT BALANCE

CHALLENGE

Ted is outnumbered four to one by the females in his family, and while he dearly loves his wife, Jackie, and their three daughters, sometimes he just needs a little respite from all that feminine energy. The couple's master bedroom is the last undecorated room in the house—full of hand-me-downs, too many florals, and no storage—and it was Jackie's idea to turn that room into a more gender-neutral place where Ted could relax in "guy style." As far as Ted was concerned, everything in the bedroom could go, except the bed—and Jackie!

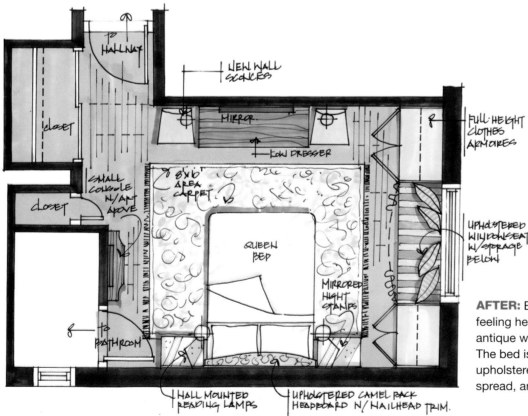

AFTER: Blue establishes the masculine feeling here, complemented by soft antique white on the cabinetry and trim. The bed is the big story, with a beautiful upholstered headboard, a crisp white spread, and stacks of accent pillows.

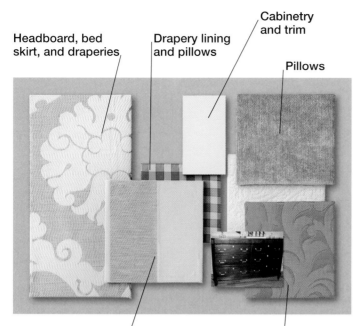

Headboard, bed skirt, and draperies

Drapery lining and pillows

Cabinetry and trim

Pillows

Roman shades and window seat

Side chairs

BEFORE: Jackie and Ted's bedroom was last on the list of rooms to be decorated, so they'd been living with its hand-me-down furniture and tired floral fabrics for most of their married life.

Elegant bow-front draperies frame a new window seat perfect for one—or two. The wide stripe on the seat cushion and Roman shade complements the damask with a more masculine geometric design, but bobble trim on the shade adds a slightly feminine detail.

SOLUTION

- To create a bedroom they both could love, I got rid of all the old furniture and fabrics and started from scratch. The room was starved for storage—in fact, with only one teeny-weeny bedroom closet, it's a miracle Ted and Jackie have stayed married for 13 years! I created a whole feature wall of new custom cabinets framing the window and added a large new dresser as well.

- Under the window between the cabinets I built a long bench with storage below.

- A new upholstered headboard, mounted on the wall with French cleats, gives the bed more presence and is high enough for Ted to lean against and read in bed.

- Color and finishes really help define the yin-and-yang character of this space. I chose a steely blue for the walls and creamy white for the trim to establish a restful but masculine tone. The color matches one of Jackie's favorite necklaces, so I know she'll like it too. Dark mahogany wood and sleek chrome finishes have a manly feel, and I balanced them with mirrored surfaces and touches of crystal to address the glamorous, feminine side of things.

STYLE ELEMENTS

- I chose a beautiful silvery blue-and-cream damask for the headboard, draperies, and bed skirt. It's a large-scale, bold pattern that's very elegant and gender-neutral, and all of the colors in the room really speak back to this fabric. For a more decidedly masculine statement, I chose stripes and checks for accent pillows, the Roman shade, and the window seat cushion. Warm pumpkin accents on pillows and two cameo side chairs add some pizzazz to the tranquil scheme.

- Recessed lights installed around the room take care of the practical side of things, and sconces and chandeliers supply intimacy and ambience. The fixture over the bed epitomizes what this room is about: It has a traditional, architectural shape that's been pared down, streamlined, and masculine, but it's outlined with crystal beads for a feminine and elegant look. The window seat gets its own pendant fixture of crystal beads, and a pair of sconces frame the dresser mirror.

- To give the window seat a cozy "nooky" feeling, I designed the draperies with a bow-front treatment and caught them up like theater curtains with fixed hold-backs.

- For the new cabinetry, I chose recessed-panel doors and drawer fronts and traditional crown molding. A bright, fresh finish balances the dark wood tones in the room. A blue glaze made from four parts glaze to one part wall color accentuates the recesses with subtle detailing.

OPPOSITE: I love mirrored bedside tables—they're elegant, formal, and practical, enlarging the sense of space. A swing-arm wall-mounted lamp on either side of the bed can be positioned for reading in bed.

BELOW: Dark woods have visual weight that anchors the silvery blue scheme, and they speak to the masculine side of the design. A pair of cameo chairs add practical extra seating but are small-scale to suit the size of the room. The fluffy pillow? A bit of fun!

URBAN SALSA

CHALLENGE

Milena and Bill are newly married 30-somethings who have just bought their first house and are redecorating, one room at a time. Their bedroom is stuck in a 1980s time warp with pink walls, yucky burgundy blinds, and old gray carpeting. The furniture . . . well, the furniture includes Milena's childhood brass bed and white lacquered pieces that have followed her from her teen years into adulthood. She's sentimentally attached to them, but Bill says no more! He's a quiet North American whose style is contemporary and urban; she's an outgoing, salsa-dancing South American who would love a sultry, spicy look. They want to blend their styles in a room they'll both enjoy.

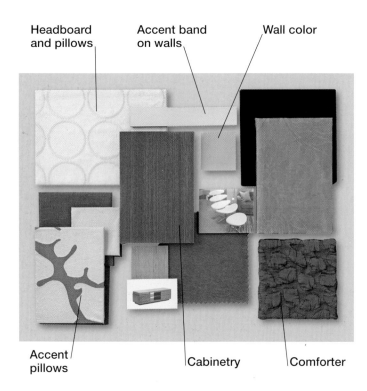

Headboard and pillows / Accent band on walls / Wall color / Accent pillows / Cabinetry / Comforter

BEFORE: With pink walls, ugly heather-burgundy shades, and old gray carpet, this room was stuck in the 1980s. The furniture had been with Milena since her teen years, but she knew it was time for it to go.

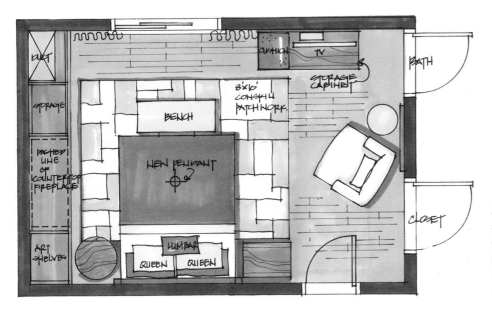

AFTER: A color scheme of smoky blue and rich dark brown puts a sultry spin on cool, contemporary style. Mirror-backed shelving in the new custom cabinetry adds depth to the room and drama to displays.

SOLUTION

- First, the practical stuff: Milena's furniture was retired to the guest room, and the old gray carpet went to the dumpster.

- In place of carpeting, I installed a pre-finished hardwood floor in a rich, dark color for a luxurious look underfoot.

- This room needed storage, especially for Bill, so I designed a whole wall of cabinetry. In the corner, the cabinet is shallow enough to fit over an ugly duct and hide it completely. The rest of the unit includes closets for clothes and dancing shoes, as well as shelves for display and open storage.

- Nothing adds romance to a room like a fireplace, and I found just the right model: a portable ethanol-burning fireplace that can be set right into the framework of the new cabinetry.

- I positioned the bed on the wall opposite the windows so it looks out onto the patio, leaving space for a lounge area with a recliner and a flat-screen TV.

- To play up the bed as the room's focal point, I designed a huge, super-modern three-part headboard that combines an upholstered band with polished wood.

LEFT: The new wall unit includes open storage below and closed cabinets above. I dressed the bed in a mix of his-and-hers fabrics: a feminine, stylized damask for her, a contemporary creamy microfiber with a circular embroidered pattern for him, and quilted, bubble-textured coverlets in brown and blue for both.

ABOVE: Three doors meant there was really only one good spot for the bed, so I turned this end of the room into a lounge area with a hip, leather-upholstered chair that is an icon of 1960s Scandinavian design (it looks like a caterpillar!). To downplay the doors, I treated them like walls and hung Bill and Milena's wedding photos on them. The door-height mirror also adds interest to this side of the room.

STYLE ELEMENTS

- Milena wanted something sexy and spicy, and Bill wanted something calm and contemporary. Spicy usually makes you think of red, but if you move spicy toward sultry, you get something moodier and more modern. I chose espresso-brown wood tones for the headboard, storage wall, and flooring, and a smoky blue for the walls and bedding.

- A wide stripe of lighter blue runs around the room in line with the upholstered band for a modern, graphic effect that unifies all the walls.

- At the windows, I hung traditional gray damask sheers and flanked them with dramatic black velvet panels.

- Strategically placed recessed halogen lights provide all-over illumination, and contemporary sconces flank the bed for reading, but the really fun fixture is the chandelier over the bed. It looks like an explosion of fireworks in metal and glass!

RIGHT: The flat-screen TV is visible from the bed as well as the recliner. Floating shelves aligned with the edges of the painted band carry the eye up the wall—right to a great photo of Milena-style shoes!

ABOVE: With crystal pendants, tiny lights, and swooping wire arms, the custom chandelier is like an explosion of fireworks, throwing a network of crazy light and shadow on the ceiling.

BELOW: This innovative portable fireplace needs no ductwork or electricity. It just drops into place and operates on ethanol, which burns clean. That's spicy!

ORGANIC MODERN

CHALLENGE

Tamara and Jeff's bedroom was stuck in the chaos of renovation, with blotchy blue walls and mismatched furniture left over from their university days. The room had too little storage (only one closet, filled with Tamara's clothes!), and all of Jeff's things were stashed in plastic bins stacked along the wall. One dinky ceiling light provided the only illumination. The couple had been in the middle of a major whole-house reno when Tamara got pregnant. Now, with a healthy baby and a whole new schedule (regular feedings, no sleep), it's time to transform the master bedroom into a calm, tranquil oasis for this young family.

BEFORE: With patched walls, mismatched furniture, and a broken window shade, this bedroom was anything but a place for soothing tranquility.

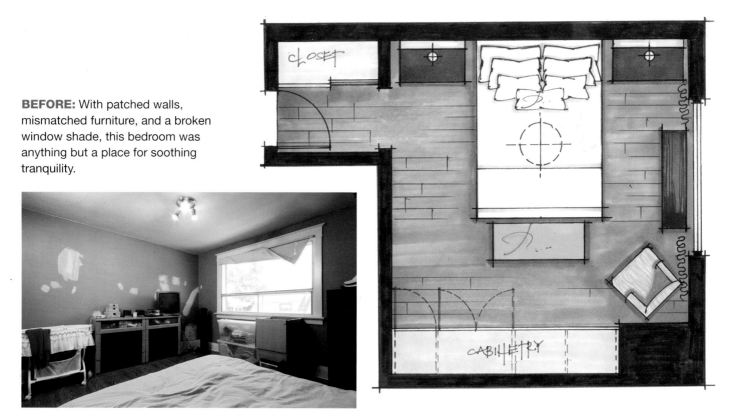

Accent pillows

Headboard graphic

Draperies and shams

Wall color

End-of-bed bench

AFTER: Clean lines and a palette of colors and textures inspired by nature create an atmosphere of restful calm.

SOLUTION

- Creating this soothing sanctuary starts with the bed, and the key word here is "natural." I've chosen an amazing eco-friendly bed system that replaces the usual inner spring polyurethane-foam construction with a Euro-style dowel foundation and layers of organic, natural rubber padding. The dowels are crafted from sustainably harvested wood, and each layer of rubber is wrapped in organic cotton gauze to protect it from wear.

- To give the room a focus, I designed a headboard that makes a big design statement: a graphic image on canvas attached to Masonite that will hang high on the wall and serve as artwork as well as a super-durable backrest.

- Storage is a must, and a quirky niche opposite the bed is the perfect spot for a custom built-in dresser with display shelves above (see page 96). As an inexpensive, time-saving alternative to an entire set of custom cabinetry, I chose ready-to-assemble storage components to fill the wall beside the niche. These cabinets will give Jeff all the storage space he'll ever need—roll-out shelves, shoe racks, baskets, and a rod for hanging shirts and pants.

- Bedside tables that incorporate drawers, floating shelves, and tall mirrors add more storage and space-expanding reflections. To keep the table surfaces free for bedtime essentials, I installed sconces through the mirrors, eliminating the need for bedside lamps.

- The room had only one tiny ceiling fixture, so in addition to the bedside sconces, I added a handsome ceiling pendant with a diffuser to soften the glow. A track of monopoint fixtures illuminates the corners and spotlights the dresser area.

OPPOSITE: A beautiful graphic of blossoms scattered on dark wood planks makes a show-stopping focal point for the room. The soft green and cream floral on the accent pillows was the jumping-off point for the room's palette of cream, bark, and celery green.

LEFT: Mounting the sconce on the bedside mirror doubles the impact of its light. The little linen shade is a small-scale version of the ceiling fixture over the bed. Natural textures of woven wood and grass add warmth to a modern space.

ABOVE: Store-bought cabinets with frosted doors fit perfectly into the niche opposite the bed. Along with a custom built-in dresser and shelves, the cabinets turn this awkward area into a practical, fully functional storage zone. A colorful composition of carved blocks brings artful color to the side wall.

STYLE ELEMENTS

- Fresh flowers inspired the finishes that would turn this disorganized, chaotic bedroom into a tranquil oasis. I found a beautiful image of blossoms and had it enlarged and transferred to canvas and applied to the Masonite headboard. The color in the throat of a fresh freesia suggested the perfect celery-green hue for the walls.

- A bedroom is really all about fabrics—at the windows, on the bed, and on seating that adds to the room's comfort. I found a beautiful cherry-blossom-floral linen that picked up on the headboard graphic and provided the jumping-off point for the room's palette of green, bark, and cream. The softly pleated linen frames the windows; lined with cotton instead of blackout lining, the draperies will glow when the sun shines through.

- Pulling out colors in the floral linen, I upholstered an end-of-the-bed bench with a soft, buttery vinyl in fresh green and covered a compact, comfy chair in a pale brown print that resembles wood grain.

- Because modern rooms can come off as cold and sterile, I selected Shaker-style cabinetry for the bedside tables and built-in dresser. This touch of tradition offsets the contemporary look of the frosted-glass doors on Jeff's new clothes cabinets and adds character.

RIGHT: A compact chair with simple lines and low arms gives Tamara a comfy place to sit and feed baby Jasmine but doesn't take up much room physically or visually.

A RELAXING REFUGE

CHALLENGE

Caterers Damon and Jodie poured all of their renovating energy into installing a professional kitchen in their new home, so when it came to turning the third-floor space into their master bedroom, they never got farther than installing floors and exposing the brick. Dust filtered through cracks in the brickwork, and the uninsulated walls kept the space freezing in winter and boiling in summer. Two large wardrobes really didn't hold much, and Damon's vast shoe collection needed a decent home! This large, dark, unsavory space was far from the romantic, rustic-chic retreat the hardworking couple needed at the end of the day.

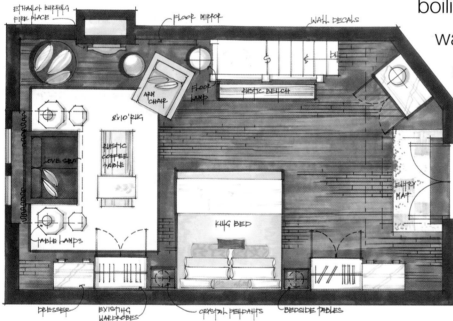

BEFORE: The large third floor had great potential as a master bedroom, but even with two large, free-standing closet units and a couple of dressers, the couple's shoe collection had no place to hide.

AFTER: Crisp white paint plays up the texture of the exposed brick, turning it into a rustic-chic backdrop for the king-size bed. A new furniture arrangement makes better use of the space, allowing for sleeping and clothing storage at one end of the attic and a cozy fireside lounge at the other.

Faux beams add architectural definition and house recessed lights for overall illumination. Lighting is critical to banishing the dark, cold feeling here, so I added spotlights over the bed, tiered pendants for bedside reading, and table lamps for task and ambient lighting in the lounge area.

ABOVE: A coat of white paint and new doors gave the large, free-standing clothing cabinets a more traditional look that better matched the Mission-style bed. Petite tables tuck in between the cabinets and the bed to hold books and bedside necessities.

SOLUTION

- The dark stained floor and dark wood bed would be staying, so the first order of business was to add light. Painting the exposed-brick wall a crisp white and the other walls a warm putty immediately brightened the space.

- Faux beams add architectural interest and provide housing for recessed lights that further banish the shadows.

- The beams also define a new, center-stage spot for the bed. Moving it from in front of the windows gives it the presence it deserves and freed up space in front of the beautiful dormer windows for a cozy lounging area.

- Moving the wardrobes uncovered the old chimney—the perfect spot for a new stainless-steel ethanol-burning fireplace! Nothing says romantic retreat like a cozy fire.

- To solve the storage problem, I repurposed the old mirror-fronted wardrobes and brought in some ordinary ready-to-assemble chests of drawers. One set of drawers was customized just for Damon's shoes!

RIGHT: I replaced the single large dark-stained dresser with store-bought three-drawer chests that I customized with new, sparkly handles and glass-covered sisal tops.

STYLE ELEMENTS

- The paneled, Mission-style headboard and footboard and the dark wood floors gave me a starting point for finishes. To balance the dark wood tones, I brought in light with white cabinetry, paint, and bedding.

- To work with the lines of the bed, I retrofitted the old mirror-fronted wardrobes with raised-panel doors and traditional-style glass panes. I gave the out-of-the-box dressers a super-high-end look by adding shiny modern pulls and sisal wallpaper capped with glass for the tops.

- Fabrics in shades of pear, moss, brown, and beige add a punch of fresh, earthy color throughout the space. Because Damon and Jodie share the bedroom with two big dogs, I selected dog-friendly fabrics in tones similar to their coats for the love seat and armchair in the lounge area.

- Tiny bedside tables blend with the wood of the headboard. To free up table space, I installed tiered pendant lamps over the side tables—a little touch of glamour against the rustic brick wall.

- I kept the window treatments clean and simple to match the rugged, rustic feeling of the exposed brick. Woven-grass blinds with blackout lining block light so Damon and Jodie can sleep late after a hard night's work. Green linen panels with a grommet edge just kiss the floor and provide softness.

OPPOSITE: A fluffy white rug anchors the seating area in front of the dormer window. Nesting side tables flank the comfy love seat—the color could be moss, or it could be Rhodesian Ridgeback! The low coffee table includes a laminated partner table that can be moved anywhere along the length of the base table. (Perfect for working jigsaw puzzles or eating dinner in front of the TV.)

RIGHT: A new stainless-steel ethanol-burning fireplace is the focal point for the lounge area. Ethanol burns clean and there's no need for venting.

The stairway to the third floor was much too narrow to hang any artwork, so I used peel-and-stick vinyl transfers in a log cross-section design to liven up the wall.

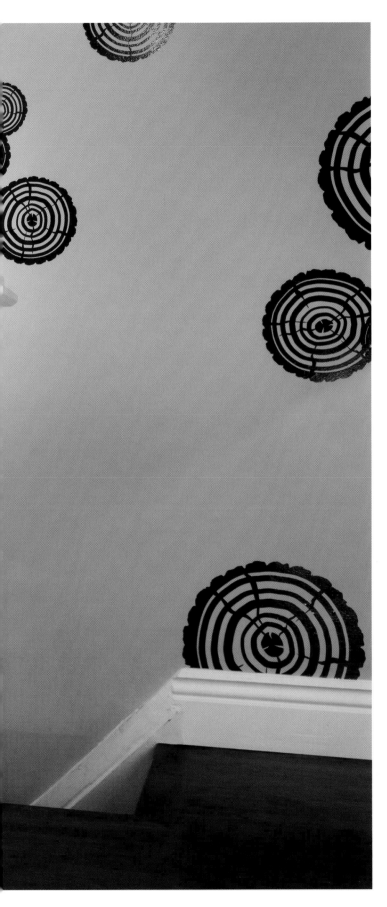

ABOVE: Something about this space just said "moose" to me. Pillow shams and decorative pillows bring color from the lounging area over to the sleeping zone. Solids in satiny and matte finishes keep the overall effect calm and quiet, but a graphic damask pattern on two feature pillows adds a feminine flourish for contrast.

HUB OF THE HOME

CHALLENGE

Designing spaces that can accommodate a wheelchair is becoming more important as better health care and new technologies help people live independently who might not have been able to before. Renovating to include an elevator and accessible spaces can make all the difference in allowing a family to live comfortably and function normally—and there's no reason those spaces can't be beautiful! One of my clients asked for my help in turning a second-floor bedroom into a wheelchair-friendly space that could serve as a comfortable gathering place for the whole family. Here's how I did it.

Drapery fabric   Pillows

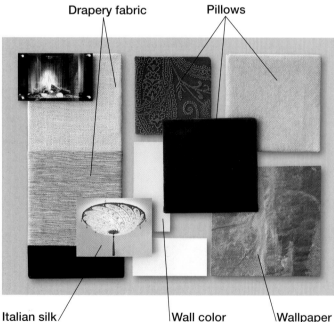

Italian silk/chandelier   Wall color   Wallpaper

BEFORE: This large room on the second floor needed to be revamped and outfitted with an elevator so that it would be wheelchair-accessible and function as the family living space for the clients and their children.

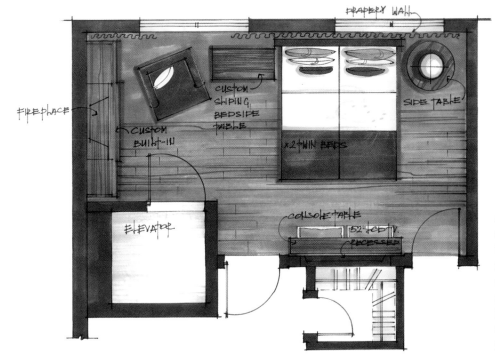

Labels in floor plan: DRAPERY WALL, FIREPLACE, CUSTOM BUILT-IN, CUSTOM SHIPING BEDSIDE TABLE, x2 TWIN BEDS, SIDE TABLE, ELEVATOR, CONSOLE TABLE, 52" LCD TV, RECESSED

AFTER: Centering the bed on the window wall allows room for a wheelchair to move easily around the space. To disguise the fact that the bed overlaps one set of windows, I installed a softly gathered fabric backdrop behind the headboard and covered the rest of the wall with a drapery panel to match those framing the remaining set of windows.

A raised gas fireplace is the centerpiece of a new wall of storage and display space. It can be enjoyed from both the lounge area and the bed.

SOLUTION

- Function came first: The best place for the elevator shaft was where the closet had been, so we took out walls to make way for it. At the other end of the room, we removed a fireplace to gain as much floor space as possible.

- To replace the lost fireplace, I designed a multifunctional custom wall unit near the elevator that combines a raised, built-in gas fireplace, dresser drawers, and display shelves. The fireplace throws out enough heat to warm the space and makes a wonderful focal point for a seating area, balancing the impact of the elevator.

- To position the bed so there would be enough room for circulation, I had to ignore the location of the windows. Not a problem: Layers of drapery create a dramatic backdrop for the bed and completely hide one set of windows. Drapery panels frame the remaining window and extend along the wall on the other side of the bed, creating a balanced, intentional look.

- On the wall opposite the bed, I installed a huge mirror that doubles as a big-screen TV (see page 115). (It's true! Super-cool technology combines an LCD TV with a mirrored surface so the television vanishes when it's turned off.)

STYLE ELEMENTS

- The client wanted the space to have a rustic, woodsy feeling. I found a beautiful hand-painted wallpaper that recalled a rocky escarpment, with tones of brown, rust, and stone. Covering the entire end wall, it balances the custom cabinetry at the opposite end of the room and inspired the color scheme for the space (see page 114).

- To ground the bed in its central location, I chose a woven-grass fabric with a wood-grain texture to hang behind the bed like a canopy. On each side, creamy raw silk panels soften the walls and act as an architectural feature.

- The client needed an ordinary hospital bed, but I didn't want it to look ordinary or like a hospital bed. I designed an upholstered, wall-mounted headboard in truffle-brown velvet to establish the feeling of a luxurious hotel suite, then dressed the bed in organic cotton bedding with a rich chocolate coverlet, snowy white blankets, and layers of pillows in cream, chocolate, and rust.

- A creamy putty color on the walls, dark walnut floors, and beautiful dark wood cabinetry enhance the earthy, manly ambience.

- The fireplace, positioned at eye level so it's visible from anywhere in the room, brings home a cottage-like feel. There's room in front of it for a chocolate-brown lounge chair and two upholstered cube seats that can be stashed under the console below the TV when they're not in use.

- A round pedestal table holds a lamp on one side of the bed. For the other side, I designed a tall table on wheels that can double as a hospital-style tray table.

- Recessed lights around the perimeter of the room wash light down the walls for overall illumination. Under-cabinet lighting spotlights objects on display on either side of the fireplace, and a hand-painted silk ceiling fixture hangs as an artistic focal point above the bed.

I designed a bedside table on wheels that doubles as a tray table. The top slides open to reveal a shallow storage space, and there's more handy storage on the shelves below. The bed proves that hospital beds don't have to look sterile. The wall-mounted upholstered headboard and layers of organic bedding in beautiful earth tones give this bed the sumptuous look of a luxury hotel bed.

ABOVE: The huge mirror opposite the bed does more than enhance the illusion of space—it's also a TV! Below the console table, block seats with cushions can be pulled out and moved over to the lounge area when needed.

LEFT: A gorgeous Italian hand-painted silk light fixture hangs like a work of art over the bed. The wall at the end of the room became a feature wall with hand-painted wallpaper that provided the starting point for the room's color scheme.

2 PERSONAL
SPACES

ANYTHING BUT PURPLE

CHALLENGE

When Tatiana and her globe-trotting family decided to settle down, she asked her brother to paint the new house in time for her arrival. Unfortunately, she forgot to specify the colors and arrived to find the interiors pulsating in shades of vivid purple. The only unpainted room was the all-white attic bedroom, which presented a few design difficulties: It had too many doors (six, to be exact!), one tiny window, lighting in all the wrong places, and a pinkish carpet. Tatiana, who normally loves color, was stuck for ideas on how to make the space hip, modern, luxurious—and anything but purple.

Wall color — Door paint — Hand-stamped wallpaper — Chaise — Window treatment

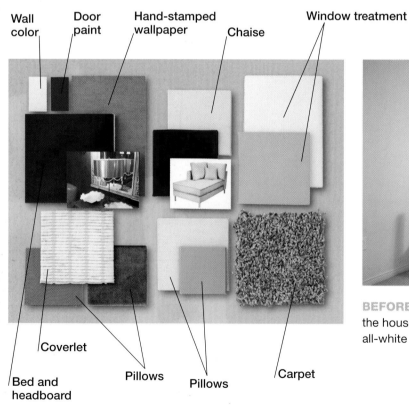

Coverlet

Bed and headboard

Pillows

Pillows

Carpet

BEFORE: An overdose of candy-store purple elsewhere in the house left Tatiana color-phobic and afraid to tackle the all-white attic bedroom.

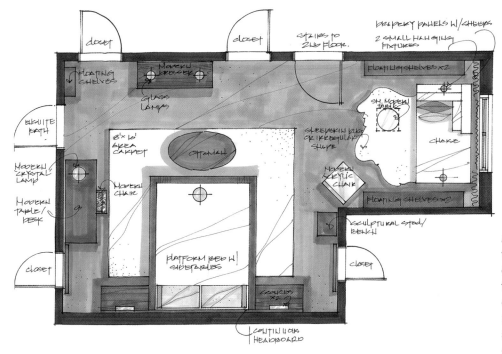

AFTER: A gorgeous bronze metallic wallpaper and a sprawling custom-designed headboard and platform bed turn one wall into a feature that defines the character of the whole space. Centered under the eaves, the bed defines the sleeping zone of this sophisticated and oh-so-relaxing attic retreat.

ABOVE: The 10-foot-long headboard includes a built-in shelf to serve as a side table on each side of the bed. Sleek ultra-modern sconces are integrated into the headboard.

SOLUTION

- I started by dividing the L-shaped room into two zones—a sleeping zone nestled under the eaves and an intimate lounge area in the window alcove.

- In the bedroom area, the only wall without doors became the feature wall, with a custom-designed 10-foot-long headboard and platform bed. The sleek, contemporary headboard incorporates shelves for bedside tables and integrated sconces for bedtime reading.

- The six doors were ordinary builder's doors with no particular character, so I transformed them into a design feature by painting them a warm chocolate brown. Then I applied full-length mirror panels to the two closet doors so they could serve as dressing mirrors. Two doors that led to storage areas were hidden behind leaning mirrors. Problem solved!

- In the lounge area I installed versatile floating shelves on both walls, and furnished the space with a comfy chaise and visually lightweight clear acrylic occasional chair.

- To give the small window more substance, I installed floor-to-ceiling sheers and overlaid them with silk drapery panels that run from wall to wall.

- Lighting is key to creating ambience and drama, but we couldn't install recessed lighting here because of the narrow crawl space above. Instead, I positioned surface-mounted halogen fixtures around the perimeter of the room and hung a sleek halogen chandelier above the bed. A fabric shade fits snugly over the fixture, and an acrylic diffuser hides the bulbs to eliminate glare. In the lounge area, super-sleek pendants spiral down from the ceiling and frame the chaise with light.

STYLE ELEMENTS

- This bedroom had to be all about calm, comfort, and relaxation—and no purple—so I chose a palette of warm, dramatic neutrals with raspberry accents for a pop of color.

- For the feature wall behind the bed, I found a stunning hand-stamped bronze wallpaper. Applied to the entire wall behind the headboard, it's like a piece of installation art that shimmers under the glow of the halogen monopoint lights.

- I painted the rest of the walls and ceiling a warm creamy-putty color to help lighten the space and emphasize the impact of the feature wall.

- A heathery charcoal-and-taupe cut-pile carpet runs throughout the space and unifies the sleeping and lounging zones. I layered a creamy shag rug over the carpet to define the bed area and gave the lounge its own dark chocolate "bear" rug to anchor the space.

- All of the wood furnishings are dark espresso brown and ebony for a sophisticated, modern look. Bronze, cream, and putty bed linens and upholstery provide a range of tones that soften the contrast between the darkest darks and lightest lights and wrap the room in quiet luxury.

OPPOSITE: I turned the window alcove into a lounge area with a cushy chaise, some floating shelves, and a clear acrylic chair. To make the small window seem more substantial, I hung floor-to-ceiling silk draperies to extend to the walls.

RIGHT: The builder doors got a major makeover with a coat of chocolate-brown paint. The two closet doors are also faced with mirrors.

LEFT: In a small area, clear acrylic furnishings provide function without taking up a lot of space visually. Floating shelves and chic, contemporary pendant lights also reduce visual clutter.

OPPOSITE: Never underestimate the power of contrasting textures to create luxury and warmth in a room wrapped in neutrals. From the lustrous sheen of silk draperies to the matte weave of the chaise upholstery, the plush softness of the area rug, and the shaggy fuzziness of the accent pillow, this minimalist lounge area radiates maximum comfort and relaxation.

ISLAND INSPIRATION

CHALLENGE

Poppy bought her dream home many years ago and planned to redecorate one room at a time. Now at last it's the bedroom's turn to be in the redecorating spotlight, and the task is leaving Poppy a little dazed. It's a huge space, with acres of pink carpet and floral wallpaper, and it has not one but two bathrooms, including a palatial one just for the tub! She'd like to replace the 1980s décor with something fresh and modern, yet reminiscent of her childhood home in the Caribbean. I'm going to surprise her with a space that's even bigger—but much more functional!

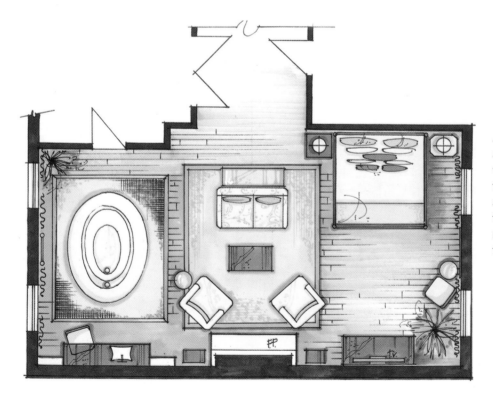

AFTER: Closing up the closet area allowed me to move the bed to that wall, so Poppy could enjoy the view of the fireplace. Super-comfy rolled-back armchairs and a 5-foot-long love seat turn the center of the once-gargantuan room into a cozy, intimate seating area in front of the fireplace.

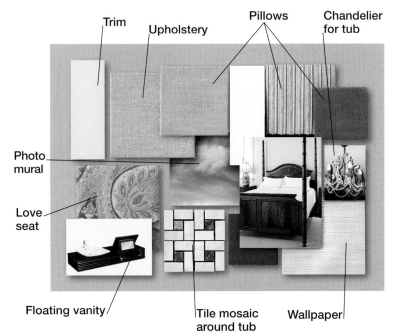

Trim
Upholstery
Pillows
Chandelier for tub
Photo mural
Love seat
Floating vanity
Tile mosaic around tub
Wallpaper

BEFORE: Not everything is pretty in pink! In this gargantuan bedroom, acres of plush pink carpet, densely patterned floral wallpaper, and dated draperies were mired in the 1980s. The handsome fireplace was never used, and all of the furniture huddled in one corner.

High-style resort hotels have nothing on Poppy's new bedroom. There's even a grand entrance (on the left) with a vestibule. A lovely area rug holds all the colors of the room and defines the lounging area in front of the fireplace as a room within the room.

SOLUTION

- Although the room was cavernous, the layout made furniture arrangement difficult, and much of the space simply wasn't functional. I began by knocking down walls to take out the incongruous tub room and closed up the wall of closets. That let me position the bed on the wall opposite the fireplace and create a new, luxurious spa area at one end of the room.

- The focal point in the en suite spa area is a spectacular, free-standing infinity-edge tub surrounded by a mosaic tile "rug." Because this kind of tub requires a lot of hot water, I installed a tankless water heater in the wall. It efficiently delivers on demand all the hot water Poppy needs.

- The spa area also features a floating vanity and huge wall mirror. Fitted with a vessel sink and a very cool stick-shift faucet, the vanity has self-closing drawers and a pop-up makeup mirror. Très chic!

- I divided the remaining area into two zones—a cozy sleeping zone and an elegant seating area anchored by the fireplace. The seating area gives the center of the room new purpose, and the bed is placed so that Poppy can see both the fireplace and the TV without needing binoculars.

- With a new remote-controlled gas insert, the fireplace is now functional *and* a focal point.

- After the dated pink carpeting was ripped out, I laid down a beautiful pre-finished, hand-scraped walnut flooring that unifies the entire area. The prominent grain of the wood has a casual look, and the dark finish is what you would find in a beach house in the tropics.

- I papered right over the old floral wallpaper with a new grass-cloth wallcovering that has a metallic foil backing. The grass cloth is very modern, but its natural texture evokes a beachy atmosphere. New, deeper crown molding has a simpler, less formal profile than the original molding and better suits the scale of the room.

ABOVE: Knocking out walls and eliminating the old marble-lined tub room created a new space for a luxurious, resort-style en suite spa. Gauzy sheers installed on a motorized track can be drawn to close off the tub area for privacy. Recessed lights wash down on the grass-cloth wall covering, highlighting its natural texture.

STYLE ELEMENTS

- Poppy loves sand, sea, sky, and all things tropical, so I knew exactly where to go for colors and textures. A palette of beiges, browns, and blues creates an easy, laid-back tranquility in the bedroom and lounge areas. In the spa area, the dark walnut tub surround and vanity pick up on the color of the floor, and the brown-and-white mosaic tile "rug" relates to both the floor and the sparkling white quartz tub deck.

- I found the perfect bed for Poppy's new tropical space: a swirled mahogany king-size four-poster with hand-carved bamboo details. It immediately says "island plantation style."

- Because the wall behind the bed should always be special, I applied a photographic mural that brings the brilliant blue tropical sky right into the room.

- Over the lounge area, I installed a fantastic fan with palm-shaped blades made from palm wicker and woven bamboo. It's guaranteed to stir up island breezes—the instruction manual says so!

- For the windows, I wanted to capture the effect of softly billowing mosquito netting, so I chose simple panels of whispery translucent sheer fabric. The same material divides the spa from the rest of the room. This privacy curtain is installed on a motorized track and can be opened and closed by remote control.

LEFT: I positioned a new credenza and large flat-screen TV on the wall opposite the end of the bed. Now Poppy can comfortably watch TV from bed and also enjoy the fireplace.

ABOVE: A king-size mahogany bed with bamboo detailing instantly invokes a tropical beach-side hotel, and the photo mural of a brilliant sky simply enhances the illusion. Beautifully detailed pillows in colors of sand and sea add layers of comfort to the bed.

OPPOSITE: I love this incredible tub! The infinity edge allows for the most luxurious soaking experience, and a crystal chandelier overhead adds elegant, feminine sparkle. Since water and wood floors don't mix, I surrounded the tub with a mosaic of tiles for a splash-proof surface.

BELOW: The vanity, designed to look like a floating shelf, includes self-closing drawers. A pair of mirrored sconces supplements the overall illumination of recessed ceiling fixtures.

HOTEL ELEGANCE

CHALLENGE

To say that Laura's house is a zoo is not much of an exaggeration. Her husband is a busy surgeon, so the job of caring for their three lively children, four cats, two dogs, two rats, two hermit crabs, one snake, and one snail (whew!) falls mostly to her. She would love to have a quiet place to retreat to at the end of the day, but at a whopping 500 square feet, her 1980s master bedroom was too big and too dated to be a welcoming oasis. It was perfect, however, for a hotel-like suite where Laura could check in for a little rest and relaxation with her devoted, hardworking hubby.

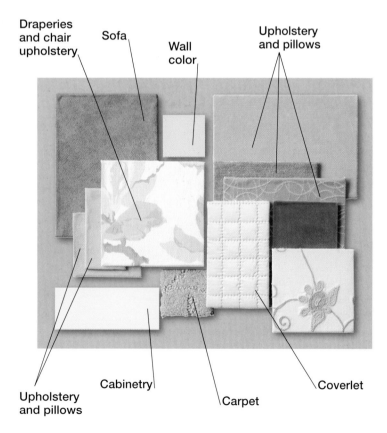

Draperies and chair upholstery · Sofa · Wall color · Upholstery and pillows · Upholstery and pillows · Cabinetry · Carpet · Coverlet

BEFORE: Acres of blue-green carpet and peach-color faux-finished walls just emphasized how dated the décor was in this enormous bedroom. The space was underutilized, and the fireplace was too small for the scale of the room.

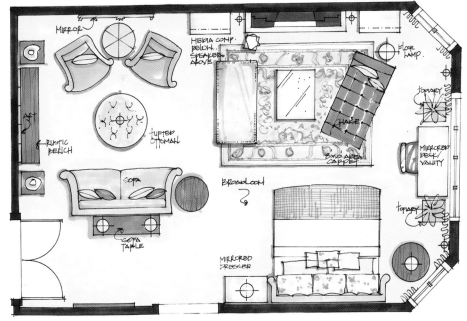

AFTER: Wrapped in warm, creamy tones with soft blue and tan accents, this expansive bedroom is now an elegant, incredibly serene retreat. Wood trim turns the once-boring vaulted ceiling into an architectural feature that adds character to the room.

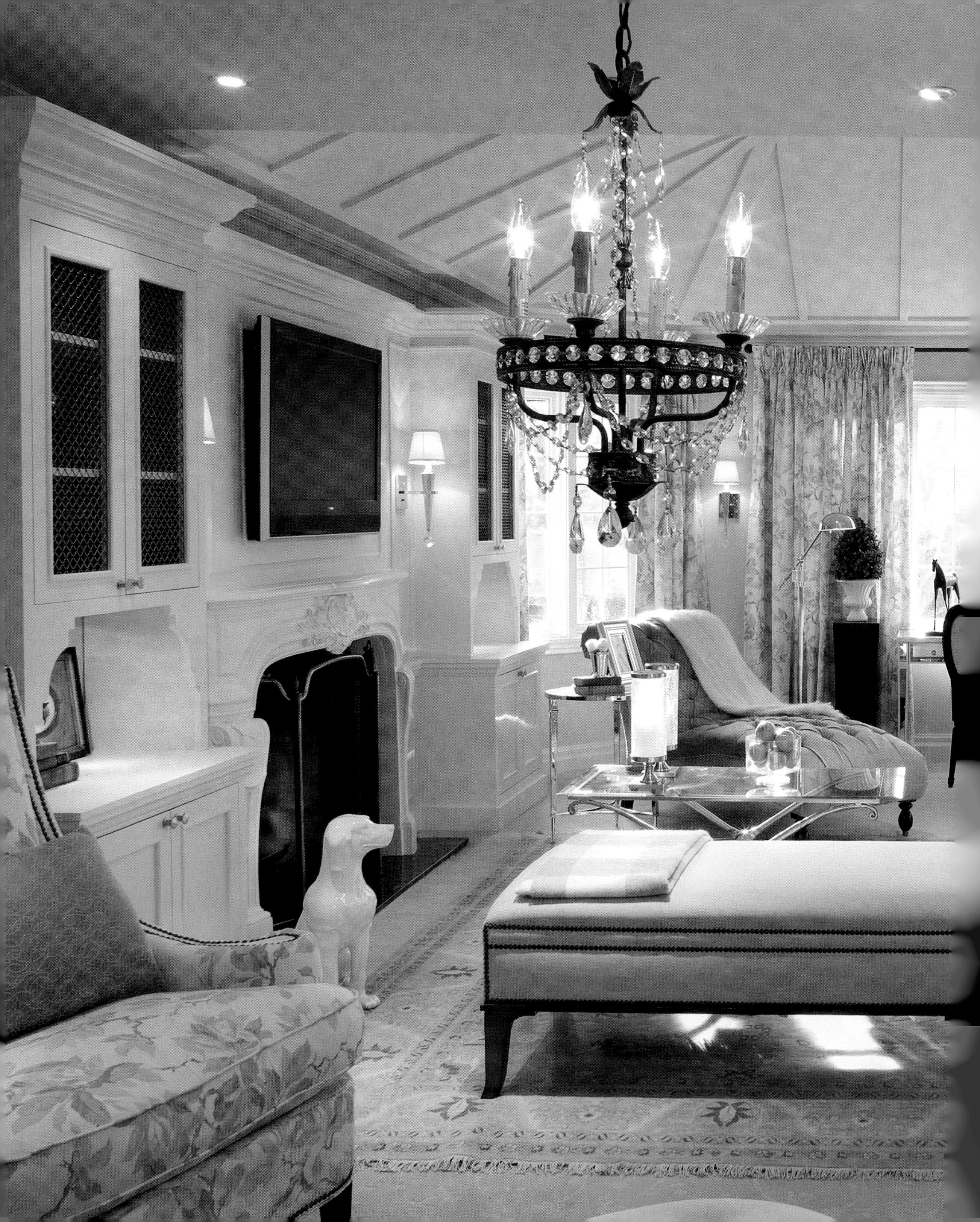

With two functional zones, one for sitting/lounging and one for sleeping/reading/writing, the 500-square-foot room feels like a high-end resort hotel—the perfect place for Laura to enjoy a little quiet time at the end of the day.

SOLUTION

- The first step in turning this vast space into an elegant oasis was to define two intimate zones: a bed/lounge area and a sitting area.

- The fireplace is the room's natural focal point but was too small to have enough impact on its own, so I flanked it with new floor-to-ceiling cabinets to give it more visual weight.

- I built out the wall above the fireplace to hold a new plasma-screen TV and placed the bed directly across from it so Laura and her husband can enjoy the fire *and* watch television in bed. The TV is on a swivel bracket and can be tilted toward the sitting area, too. (Now all they need is room service!)

- Trim and wood strapping applied to the soaring vaulted ceiling make this once-boring, unnoticed area an interesting architectural feature.

- A beautiful new upholstered headboard gives the bed more importance and balances the fireplace on the other side of the room. End tables, a chaise, and a mirrored desk/vanity fill out this zone.

- I furnished the sitting area with a comfy sofa, two chairs, and an ottoman. While this room certainly didn't need the illusion of more space, a giant mirror leaning against the wall helps bounce more light around and adds a feeling of grandeur.

OPPOSITE: The mirrored desk in front of the window lets Laura enjoy the view while she's writing a note (or maybe penning her memoirs—*15 Is Enough*?). It's also the perfect element to bring the light in and bounce it farther into the room.

LEFT: This headboard, a design called "Giselle" from my collection, is inspired by a wing chair. Upholstered in soft beige fabric, it says "Come cuddle." A carved leafy architectural element on a floating shelf crowns the bed with a traditional flourish.

ABOVE: The graceful, traditional fireplace now has the visual weight to anchor the bed/sitting area, thanks to a pair of hutch-style cabinets, a new over-mantel, and applied panel moldings on the slivers of wall that flank the fireplace. Crown molding ties the cabinets, over-mantel, and intervening wall spaces into a single unit.

STYLE ELEMENTS

- Laura's tastes are traditional, so I chose white-painted MDF (medium-density fiberboard) cabinets with mesh fronts and traditional crown molding to flank the plaster fireplace. Painting the over-mantel to match the fireplace emphasizes them as a unit and helps bring the fireplace into scale with the room.

- To create the tranquil atmosphere Laura longed for, I chose a quiet, traditional color scheme of cream, fawn, wheat, and tan. I replaced the ugly blue-green carpeting with a wheat-color carpet embossed with a subtle floral pattern.

- The outdated peachy faux finish on the walls disappeared under a lighter tone of the carpet's wheat color. The ceiling is an even lighter tone of that same wheat, creating a low-contrast envelope of quiet neutral hues—the key to a serene, soothing environment.

- Fabrics bring in contrasting colors, starting with a beautiful nature-inspired floral fabric that introduces notes of glacier blue, fawn, and tan. These hues make their way onto accent pillows and the bed coverlet as solids and geometrics. The colors all have the same tonal quality so nothing is jarring, but rather relaxing, restful, and soothing. The floral frames the beautiful view out the windows and repeats on the chairs in the sitting area, helping tie the two zones together. For the sofa I chose a hard-wearing, heavy-duty, caramel-color microfiber that's pet-friendly.

- Lighting in this room is as much about mood and atmosphere as it is about function. For the vaulted ceiling, I chose a very simple drum fixture with a linen shade and a diffuser to eliminate glare from the bulbs. In the sitting area, a gorgeous traditional chandelier with beading and crystal drops hangs low over the ottoman—a dramatic and unexpected way to bring light into the middle of the room. The chrome sconces have a clean, tapered shape that brings in a modern touch with a little crystal element at the bottom for sparkle. Under-shelf lighting in the cabinets adds depth and interest.

LEFT: This shapely tufted chaise, upholstered in an elegant beige velvet, is the perfect place to stretch out and read or nap. To keep the room's design from being too stuffy, I paired traditional shapes with sleek metal pieces that update classic styles. The sconces between the windows hang lower than usual for a more intimate feeling.

ABOVE: The sofa and chairs from my collection update classic designs with clean, graceful lines and low scrolled arms that say "Come on and sit down." The art installation, a grid of shaped blocks covered in silver leaf, shakes up traditional style with a high-end, super-contemporary statement on the end wall.

BELOW: A gorgeous crystal chandelier hangs over the ottoman to anchor the seating area. I leaned an oversize mirror against the wall to bounce light from the recessed ceiling fixtures and the chandelier back into the room.

C'EST MAGNIFIQUE!

CHALLENGE

Veronique and her family recently emigrated from France to North America and have just moved into a large, traditional-style home. Between their own demanding jobs and their girls' activities, however, she and her husband, Eric, have had no time to make the house reflect their personal style. The master bedroom has a vaulted ceiling and a wall of beautiful windows, but the room was so beige, bland, and boring that these features didn't make much of an impact. Veronique wanted the room to be *magnifique, élégant, et belle,* a sanctuary where she and Eric could read in bed and spend quality time together.

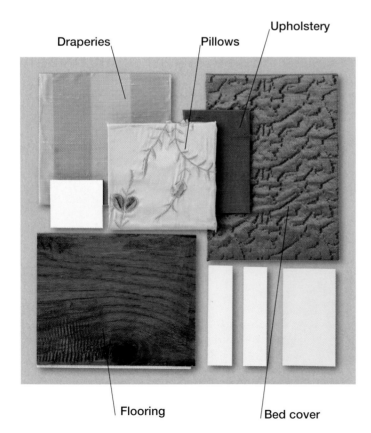

Draperies Pillows Upholstery

Flooring Bed cover

BEFORE: A study in bland beige and white, this bedroom would put a person to sleep out of boredom. Veronique and her husband led such busy lives that they simply didn't have time to put any personality into the space.

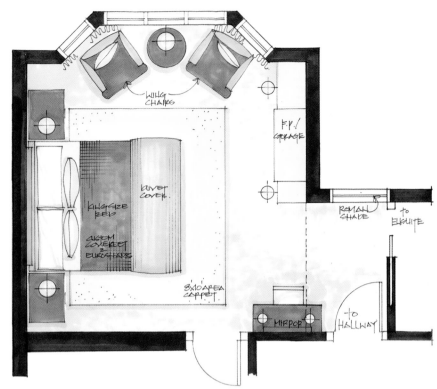

Labels in floor plan:
- WING CHAIRS
- F.P. / GARAGE
- KINGSIZE BED
- DUVET COVER
- CUSTOM COVERLET & EUROSHAMS
- ROMAN SHADE
- to ENSUITE
- 8x10 AREA CARPET
- MIRROR
- to HALLWAY

AFTER: Architectural details add character to once-bland walls, and a palette of cocoa, taupe, gold, and blue transforms boring beige into blissfully *belle.* French design inspired the curvy, antique-gold arms and embellishments on the custom chandelier.

ABOVE: Custom cabinetry built from heavy-duty medium-density fiberboard encases the new fireplace and TV cubby. Elegant little sconces add some sparkle and shine.

SOLUTION

- The high ceiling and big windows had potential, but the room was lacking architectural interest. I installed crown molding to separate the walls from the ceiling and detailed the walls with panel molding—*et voilà!* Instant traditional European character!

- Veronique wanted flooring that reminded her of Versailles—beautiful wood rather than humdrum carpeting. So it was *au revoir* to the old wall-to-wall carpet and *bonjour* to a pre-finished wide-plank flooring that looks antique.

- Nothing says *magnifique* quite like a fireplace. On the wall adjacent to the windows I installed a new gas insert fireplace with a gorgeous cast-stone mantel and surround. The gas insert is rated for small spaces, with a heat output of 11,000 BTUs, so it will keep the room cozy and romantic but not too warm. The cast-stone surround arrives in sections and is assembled on-site. It looks just like a hand-carved limestone fireplace you would see in an old chateau.

- Romance for women means a fireplace. Romance for men . . . a TV. Eric wanted to be able to watch television in bed, but Veronique didn't want to see it, so I designed custom cabinetry to surround the fireplace and hide the TV above.

- The high ceiling called for something dramatic in the way of lighting. I designed the perfect chandelier in an elegant traditional style that's in scale with the room, combining antique-gold arms and lots of crystals.

- Gorgeous new sconces add a little bit of shine to the fireplace wall, and lamps place light around the room for reading and task lighting.

RIGHT: The cast-stone fireplace surround offers the look and character of hand-carved limestone at a fraction of the cost. Above the mantel, a painting of Mont-St-Michel decorates the doors of the television cabinet in homage to a place that's important to Veronique and Eric.

STYLE ELEMENTS

- Fabrics bring in the elegance and luxury that this French-inspired room needs. The whole scheme starts with an exquisite French blue silk shot through with a taupey-brown embroidered floral design. It will appear only on accent pillows, but it provides the cue for a luscious gold-and-taupe striped silk for the draperies, a cocoa-brown coverlet in a modern, crinkly texture, cocoa upholstery on the chairs, and a yummy warm beige upholstered headboard.

- A beautiful blue, cocoa, and cream rug anchors the bed and sums up the color scheme.

- At the windows, I removed the shutters from the high clerestory windows. Light control really was not an issue, and I wanted to emphasize the architecture. Down below, beautiful silk draperies soften the windows and frame them with columns of color.

- Veronique and Eric have a personal connection to Mont-St-Michel in Normandy, so I had an artist paint a view of this amazing abbey and mounted it on the door of the TV cabinet. When the door is closed, they have artwork; when the door is open, the television is revealed.

- I chose lustrous dark wood bedside and accent tables to anchor all the neutral tones. The scrolled and saber shapes of the table legs reference classic nineteenth-century French styles and bring a little of the old country into the new home.

LEFT: This exquisite little vanity and its antique-gold chair are pure French. I love the way the mirrored surface reflects light, and it's the ideal place to show off Veronique's collection of perfume bottles.

ABOVE: The upholstered headboard is perfect for reading in bed. When I laid out the panel moldings, I was careful to make sure the center panel was wide enough to frame the new headboard. I then divided the remaining wall space into two equal rectangles. A line of identically framed prints above the bed fills the space for a finished look.

HELLO, HOLLYWOOD!

CHALLENGE

Donna's bedroom had been decorated 20 years earlier and hadn't changed since. Foil wallpaper that was all the rage at the time still covered one wall, and the carpet was original. She was tired of the color scheme and the furniture. Newly single and embarking on a new life, Donna is ready for a new bedroom. And the best part is that I have carte blanche! The only thing that has to stay is an upholstered ottoman that her pups Lucy and Ralph use to hop up on the bed.

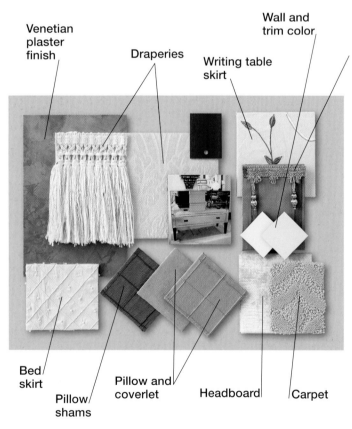

Venetian plaster finish · Draperies · Writing table skirt · Wall and trim color · Trim for table skirt topper · Bed skirt · Pillow shams · Pillow and coverlet · Headboard · Carpet

BEFORE: Donna's bedroom was a perfect time capsule of 1980s style. Foil wallpaper, sculpted carpeting, and antiqued green furniture had been stylish then, but were tired and dated now.

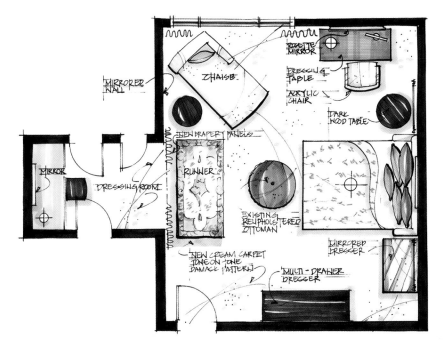

The floor plan is labeled with the following notes:

- MIRRORED WALL
- CHAISE
- ROSETTE MIRROR
- DRESSING TABLE
- ACRYLIC CHAIR
- DARK WOOD TABLE
- MIRROR
- DRESSING ROOM
- NEW DRAPERY PANELS
- RUNNER
- EXISTING REUPHOLSTERED OTTOMAN
- MIRRORED DRESSER
- NEW CREAM CARPET TONE-ON-TONE DAMASK PATTERN
- MULTI-DRAWER DRESSER

AFTER: A rich Venetian plaster finish in velvety plum makes a dramatic backdrop for a bed worthy of a starlet. Lots of mirrored surfaces and a 1930s-inspired chandelier add plenty of glamour and sparkle.

SOLUTION

- I wanted to give Donna a luxurious new bedroom that offered a new take on the golden era of Hollywood. That started with an elegant new headboard that looks like a button-tufted wing chair.

- For the wall behind the bed, I chose a layered Venetian plaster paint treatment to replace the foil wallpaper.

- I ripped out the old carpet and installed a new cut-and-looped pile carpet for plush, toe-tickling comfort.

- The drywall valance at the window needed to stay because it hides the drapery mechanics, but it needed a shot of style. Nailing a 4-inch-deep crown molding at the ceiling along the valance and around the room adds a dressy architectural element.

- New recessed lighting sheds flattering light that highlights the new finishes and fabrics. An Art Deco–inspired crystal chandelier that picks up on the design in the carpet hangs over the bed.

RIGHT: The tufted headboard evokes a wing chair and is designed to cradle Donna in comfort. The wall treatment started with a base coat of paint, followed by two coats of plum-tinted plaster, and finished with an iridescent top coat.

ABOVE: Slipcovering a desk with beautiful fabrics is an easy way to give an old table or writing desk an entirely new life. This table was custom-made for Donna, with two sets of shelves hiding behind the kick-pleated embroidered silk skirt. A glass top protects the blue silk topper and provides a hard surface for writing.

STYLE ELEMENTS

- Venetian plaster is a multi-step treatment that gives walls a lot of depth with a rich, textured finish. I chose a yummy plum color for Donna's bedroom. A violet base coat, followed by two coats of plum-tinted plaster and a top coat of iridescent purple, creates a stunning feature wall.

- For the remaining walls and the carpet, damask draperies, headboard, and chaise, I chose shades of ivory, cream, pearl, and white. The contrast plays to the beautiful purple wall but keeps it from feeling overbearing.

- The custom headboard, upholstered in antique velvet, cradles pillows with reversible covers in plum and blue silk. The comforter is reversible too, pairing blue and fuchsia.

- The pups' ottoman got a brand-new look with deep purple upholstery that punctuates the plum and blue silk accent pillows.

- Every starlet needs a writing desk to pen her memoirs, so I created a custom desk using open shelving units and slipcovered it in a beautiful embroidered silk. The pleats lift at the corners to reveal the shelves. An incredible trim of silver pendants edges the watery blue silk topper, which I capped with glass to give Donna a firm surface for writing.

- For a bit of movie magic, mirrors add sparkle and light, reflecting natural light by day and lamplight at night. I propped one large, etched mirror on the writing desk and leaned an oversize mirror against the wall behind the chaise. A sleek, 1930s-style mirrored dresser serves as a bedside table, and of course, the starlet's decorative mirrored star glitters over the bed.

OPPOSITE: Every Hollywood diva needs an overstuffed chaise to recline on. The drywall valance along the window wall needed an architectural transition, so I nailed crown molding to the ceiling around the room. Damask tone-on-tone draperies dress the windows and also create a sense of entry to the dressing room.

BELOW: In the dressing area off the bedroom, a 1930s-inspired dressing table and layered mirrors add an element of elegance.

ECO-CHIC

CHALLENGE

With inadequate lighting, out-of-scale furniture, and no separation of public and private space, Earl's third-floor attic bedroom didn't make the grade when it came to style and function. Not only was this his bedroom and home office, it was also the path his friends had to take from the stairs to the balcony, where he liked to entertain on warm summer evenings. But this was no ordinary redecorating project. As a dedicated high-school science teacher, Earl wanted to inject some eco-friendly design that demonstrates just how great "green" can be!

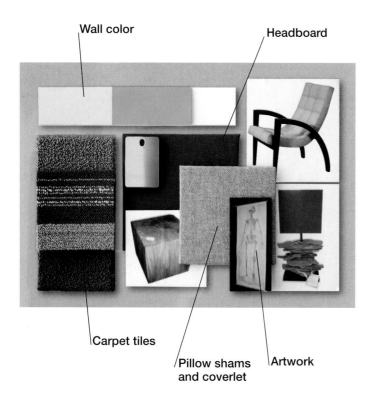

Wall color

Headboard

Carpet tiles

Pillow shams and coverlet

Artwork

BEFORE: This attic bedroom was lacking in the personality department, and as the only access to the balcony, where Earl likes to entertain friends on warm summer evenings, it couldn't pass the style test for a combination public-private space.

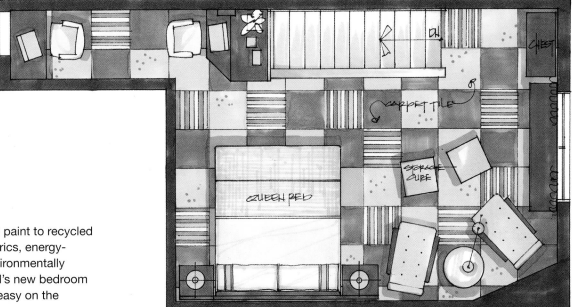

AFTER: From low-VOC paint to recycled carpet tiles, organic fabrics, energy-saving lighting, and environmentally friendly furnishings, Earl's new bedroom is easy on the eye and easy on the planet.

SOLUTION

- To better define the room's functions, I divided the space into sleeping, sitting, and office zones. Moving the bed closer to the closet freed up space for a sitting area near the balcony doors. Now when guests come up the stairs to go outdoors, they don't feel like they're walking right through Earl's bedroom.

- The room needed a focal point, so I designed a dramatic upholstered headboard and floating side tables backed with tall mirrors to anchor the space. Instead of hardwood, I used a low-formaldehyde MDF with a dark wood veneer. MDF (medium-density fiberboard) is made from the leftovers of wood processing, and the environmentally friendly type uses formaldehyde-free glues. The same material was used to build the shelves in the office nook.

- To give the walls some character, I coated them with a low VOC (volatile organic compound) paint in a beautiful, restful shade of blue. Traditional paints emit VOCs over time, and the effects are unhealthy for both people and the planet, so a low- or no-VOC alternative definitely meets Earl's standards for green design!

- Because Earl wanted to minimize his use of air conditioning, I installed a stainless-steel ceiling fan. It will not only cool the attic in summer but also helps distribute heat more efficiently in winter, cutting Earl's energy use year-round.

- Flooring was the biggest challenge, but after intensive research I found some terrific carpet tiles that are made from recycled materials. They're low in VOCs and toxic dyes, and the company will even pick them up and recycle them when you want to replace them. I chose a mix of striped and solid tiles and laid them out to create the effect of a floor rug surrounded by solid color.

- For lighting, I specified energy-saving CFL light bulbs for the bedside tables and ceiling fan fixture, and for the track lights, super-efficient LEDs. Incandescent lights gobble up 60 watts of energy to the 6 to 8 watts of an LED, and LEDs can last up to 10 years—a great way to lower your carbon footprint!

OPPOSITE: A new seating group separates the bed from the door to the balcony, creating a sense of public space for guests coming up the stairs. The carpet tiles are made of recycled materials with low VOCs and minimal use of toxic dyes and can be recycled themselves. The lounge chairs meet the earth-friendly standard, too: They're stuffed with a soy-based foam.

ABOVE: I dressed the bed with organic cottons that are made with no bleaches and no harsh dyes. The dramatic headboard is built with low-formaldehyde medium-density fiberboard covered in dark veneer. It's upholstered in chocolate-brown hemp, a low-maintenance crop that consumes little water, needs no pesticides, and is very earth-friendly.

STYLE ELEMENTS

- I chose chocolate-color hemp to upholster the headboard. Hemp is a low-maintenance crop that needs little water and no pesticides, so it's an excellent choice for an organic, environmentally sound fabric. I used the same fabric in a creamy color for grommet-topped panels at the doors to the balcony.

- For the bedding, what else but organic cottons? The soft blue, tan, and cocoa hues pick up the colors in the striped carpet tiles and offer a soothing, refreshing contrast to the dark brown headboard.

- Lounge chairs stuffed with a soy-based foam instead of the standard polyurethane foams are on the cutting edge of eco-sensitive furniture production.

- For artwork, I hung a vintage print of a skeleton—it's recycled and it nods to Earl's subject of science.

ABOVE: The stainless-steel ceiling fan helps keep the attic cooler in summer but also redistributes warm air in winter, helping cut down on energy use.

OPPOSITE: A skinny dormer offers just enough space for a small office. Woven blinds made from bamboo, reed, and grass provide light control at this little window and at the balcony doors.

RIGHT: Custom shelving on the stairwell bulkhead includes a box where I "planted" bamboo sticks to serve as a divider screen for the office area. Bamboo is one of the fastest-growing grasses on Earth, and the sculptural stalks make a great natural accent.

SUITE RETREAT

CHALLENGE

Jenn and her husband have moved from a small town to the big city, and they have lots of friends and family who come to visit. They would love to have a comfortable, welcoming guest room to make their visitors feel at home—in particular, Jenn would like to have a place that feels like a high-end hotel suite for her girlfriends when they arrive for twice-yearly, shop-til-you-drop weekend extravaganzas. The problem was that the only available spot for this suite retreat was a cluttered, unfinished basement storage room with blue-green concrete walls and one tiny window.

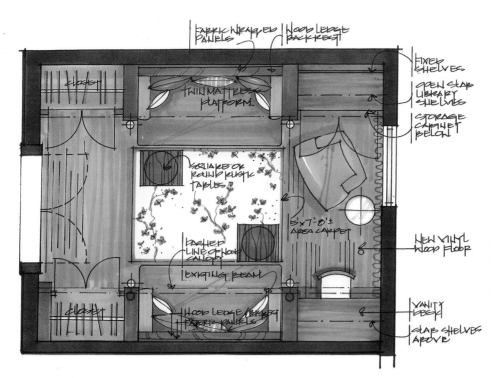

BEFORE: Once a hobbyist's workshop, the dark, unfinished basement in this 1950s house had become a disorganized, underutilized storage room next to the laundry. Jenn and her husband needed a guest room for their many out-of-town visitors. Could this room fill the bill?

AFTER: Luxuriously upholstered daybeds nestle into matching custom-built nooks on opposite sides of the room, which I widened by stealing 2 feet from the adjacent laundry room. Glamorous iridescent draperies soften the end wall and cover the small window, totally disguising the fact that this room is mostly below ground level.

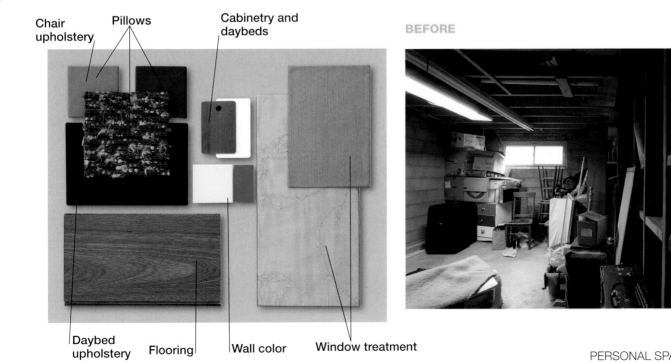

Chair upholstery

Pillows

Cabinetry and daybeds

Daybed upholstery

Flooring

Wall color

Window treatment

ABOVE: The daybed nook is almost like a room within a room, enclosed with wood walls and canopy. A beautiful upholstered panel serves as artwork on the back wall. The bulkhead above hides a trough with three under-cabinet lighting fixtures that can toggle to direct light as desired. The large closet on the right can be used by guests or family.

OPPOSITE: Swing-arm sconces allow light to be directed where it's needed for reading or lounging.

SOLUTION

- The storage room was a little too narrow, but in the world of design, stealing is 100-percent legal—stealing space, that is! I had to steal 2 feet from the laundry room, which required replacing the centered load-bearing support post with two posts that would be hidden inside the walls of a new daybed nook. We also added a bulkhead along each long wall to handle the new recessed lighting fixtures.

- Drywall applied over the concrete block and the new walls banished the subterranean feeling. I also closed up the old door and created a grand entrance with French doors centered on the new space.

- Pre-finished dark wood laminate flooring unifies the space with a rich, warm look. The click-together system is perfect for installing over a slightly uneven concrete floor.

- The *pièce de résistance* of this new space is two wood-clad nooks that feel like cozy little rooms within the room—a bit like a luxury sleeper car on the Orient Express! Floor-to-ceiling walls enclose the platform daybeds, which have custom-built backrests.

- Custom-built closets on one side of each nook provide storage space for guests' clothing or for the family's out-of-season clothes.

- On the other side of one nook I tucked a desk and shelf into the corner. It can double as an office for Jenn and a vanity for guests. In the opposite corner, shelves and a cabinet provide more space for storage and display.

- The key to banishing the basement blues is lighting. I installed recessed fixtures around the perimeter of the room to kiss the walls with light. Inside each nook, the bulkhead stops short of the back wall to create a trough where I installed three long under-cabinet fixtures like you'd use in a kitchen. The lights can be toggled to direct the light toward the back wall or down on the display shelf below. Moody accent lighting above the corner shelves adds luxurious intimacy, and swing-arm sconces on the walls of each nook serve as adjustable reading lamps.

STYLE ELEMENTS

- I chose a dark, chocolate-color wood for all of the cabinetry to create a rich, luxurious look and unify the space. A light, neutral color on all the walls and ceiling plays up the warmth of the cabinetry.

- The small window was a dead giveaway that this was a basement, so I completely masked the entire elevation with luxurious organza-embroidered satin draperies. This gorgeous fabric is flanked by gold satin panels that extend to the corners. It's now a feature wall worthy of being in the direct line of sight from the new French doors.

- For the daybed cushions and backrests, I chose a chocolatey velvet that picks up on the woodwork. The daybed seat is an ordinary twin mattress upholstered with a removable cover that slips off when it's time for bed. Accent pillows in a sophisticated palette of taupe, loganberry, and pumpkin add a punch of exciting color.

- Every guest room needs guest seating. I brought in a comfortable modern armchair and upholstered it in the same pumpkin hue as the daybed bolsters. The color repeats on the wood-block occasional tables to play up the warm, welcoming effect.

- For artwork, I upholstered wood panels with the same fabulous embroidered organza that hangs at the windows and attached them to the back walls of the nooks. Illuminated by the accent lights hidden behind the bulkhead, the fabric adds shimmery softness to balance all the hard surfaces.

OPPOSITE: A desk and shelf tucked into one corner can serve as office space for the family until guests arrive. Then it can be cleared off to serve as a dressing table for company.

LEFT: In the corner opposite the desk, a cabinet and shelves provide storage and display space. The shelves stop 6 inches short of the wall so that the accent lighting in the bulkhead can shine down and illuminate all of the shelves and the cabinet top.

3 ROOMS FOR KIDS

HIGH-TECH AND TOTALLY COOL

CHALLENGE

Nicolas is one great teenager—at age 13, he's a hardworking entrepreneur, a top student, and a role model for his younger twin brothers. His parents feel that he has more than earned his own grown-up bedroom and have agreed to let him take over his grandmother's old suite in the basement. Her antiques and dusty rose décor didn't quite suit his style, though, and they asked me to help make this space one super-cool hangout for Nicolas and friends.

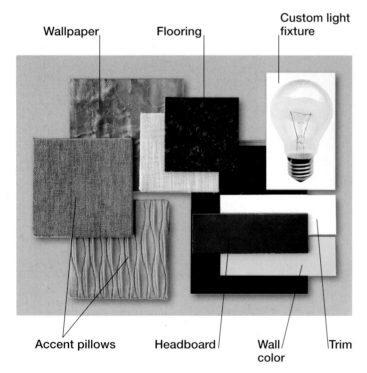

Wallpaper   Flooring   Custom light fixture

Accent pillows   Headboard   Wall color   Trim

BEFORE: Paneled walls painted pink, a lone fluorescent ceiling fixture, and cabbage-rose décor had suited Grandma but really didn't work for a teenage boy.

PLASMA TV.

MEDIA
CABINET

DAY
BED

CUSTOM
LIGHT
FIXTURE

QUEEN
BED

BENCHY
COFFEE TABLE

QUARTZ
WORK
STATION

MODERN LEATHER CHAIR

LEATHER FLOOR
TILES

AFTER: An incredible wallpaper that looks like distressed, rusted metal covers one entire wall in Nicolas's new basement bedroom. The flooring, made of recycled leather embossed with a crocodile-skin pattern, ups the cool quotient exponentially!

SOLUTION

- First I insulated the walls for heat and sound (anticipating the decibel levels of teenage music) and laid new subflooring over the original concrete floor. The subfloor provides insulation and a moisture barrier for the new plank flooring.

- I divided the room into zones for sleeping, socializing, and homework. On the window wall, a long work surface links two custom units that fill the entire end wall and provide tons of closed and open storage.

- I centered Nicolas's bed on the wall at the opposite end of the room and flanked it with custom dressers that double as nightstands.

- In the center of the room, a sleeper sofa, a couple of sleek, contemporary chairs, and an equally contemporary coffee table give Nicolas and his friends a hip-and-happenin' place to hang out and watch TV on the wall-mounted flat-screen television.

OPPOSITE: Beautiful custom cabinetry flanks the window and the work station, which is outfitted with a new computer and mixing station and all kinds of fun gadgets for Nicolas. Puck lights installed in the shelf below the window illuminate the work surface, while recessed lights in the ceiling highlight the wood and wallpaper finishes.

ABOVE: The sleeper sofa is covered in a blue-gray menswear fabric that pulls out the steely gray hue in the wallpaper. The wood-and-chrome coffee table speaks to the mix of metals and warm woods that play off each other in the room, and it's sturdy enough to support several pairs of teenage feet.

BELOW: Leather upholstery and taller legs update the famous LCW chair designed in 1945 by Charles and Ray Eames. Details like the leather-wrapped metal hardware on the cabinetry add to the masculine feel in the room and give it longevity—this is a room Nicolas won't soon outgrow.

STYLE ELEMENTS

- Nicolas loves gadgets, electronics, and mixing music, so I chose finishes and fabrics that would make this room high-tech and rock 'n' roll down to the last detail. For flooring I used a fantastic, super-cool recycled leather product embossed to resemble crocodile skin. The tones of black and brown in the leather make a dramatic base for the rest of the room.

- I turned one long wall into a feature with a spectacular handcrafted wallpaper that looks like rusted galvanized metal. It really sets the style of the room with a sort of glamour-grunge vibe, and it gives the cue for all the colors in the fabrics and the cool, steely blue I chose for the remaining walls.

- For the homework and music-mixing station, I installed a curved quartz countertop. The quartz is timeless and hard-wearing, and its mottled gray color picks up on the floor and the wallpaper. The curved shape offers a more social configuration than a straight edge would—Nicolas and a friend or two can sit here together and play video games or work on their laptops.

- The warm wood of the custom cabinets balances all the cool, metallic finishes, but even the cabinets have masculine details with leather-wrapped hardware.

- I kept Nicolas's bed and painted the headboard a steely gray-blue. For a really cool feature over the bed, I installed a one-of-a-kind light fixture, a ceiling-mounted box with 16 bulbs hanging from it on black wires.

- The bedside tables anchor open shelves backed with mirrors that bounce light and views back into the room.

OPPOSITE: A gold bed skirt helps set the bed off against the dark floor, and the striped duvet brings in some middle tones to tie the darks and lights together. The dramatic light feature is mounted to the ceiling, with individual wires threaded through an aluminum bar to keep the bulbs separated.

BELOW: Artwork that refers to Nicolas's many odd jobs in the neighborhood leans against the wall above the dresser.

SHARED SPACE

CHALLENGE

Fifteen-year-old Michael got permission two years ago to take over the basement as his own personal "guy space." Well, not exactly take over—in addition to housing his bedroom and study area, the basement still has to work as a family room, too. He would love to have a big-screen TV, a place to do his homework, and room for his friends to stay over when they visit. My job is to create a space that works for Michael in the short term and for his family in the long term—without building any walls that would permanently alter the space.

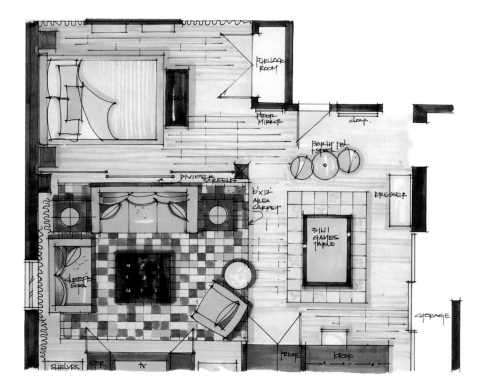

AFTER: A canvas panel on tension rods now divides the family room from Michael's bedroom. New acoustical ceiling tiles create the effect of a coffered ceiling. I installed track lights throughout the space to spotlight display areas and provide overall light. Table lamps supply task lighting.

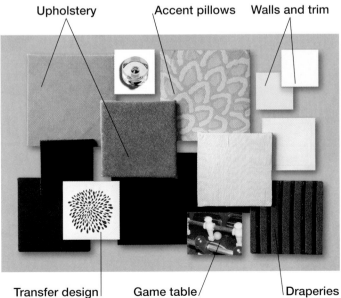

Upholstery

Accent pillows

Walls and trim

Transfer design

Game table

Draperies

BEFORE: Michael's parents had installed laminated flooring and acoustical ceiling tiles to finish the basement for Michael's use, but they couldn't decide how to complete the space so it could give the teenager the privacy he needed and still serve as a family room.

SOLUTION

- The wood laminate flooring had recently been installed, but I scrapped just about everything else. To update the existing T-bar ceiling system, I replaced the busy waffle-style acoustical tiles with streamlined squares that have a more modern look.

- Because the large space had to serve multiple functions, I identified zones for the bedroom, the family area, and a games/study area. To divide the bedroom from the family room, I installed a unique temporary divider system using large canvas panels.

- In Michael's bedroom area, a hefty new queen-size bed is the focal point. This 6-foot-tall teen had been sleeping in a twin-size bed for long enough and needed room to stretch! Tall, narrow bookshelves double as bedside tables and storage space.

- Along one entire wall, I installed a really cool display and storage system of laminated wood. It's completely customizable, with a grid of metal-lined holes; dowel-like metal brackets snap into the holes, and you can rest heavy-duty acrylic shelves on them or attach picture hooks or clips for hanging book bags or sports equipment. Any unused holes function as decoration.

- On the other side of the canvas divider, I set up the family area with a comfy 56-inch queen sleeper sofa and 79-inch regular sofa so Michael's friends have a place to crash.

- The focal point of this area is, of course, the large flat-screen TV and media center. Because a television like this can be overwhelming, I like to integrate it into dark-toned cabinetry. When the TV is off, the screen blends in with the dark wood, and when it's on, the dark wood accentuates it. This media center includes surround-sound speakers, components for playing video games, and tons of storage.

- In the corner beside a custom storage cabinet and mini-fridge, I built a desk for Michael's study zone. I also designated this end of the room as a game zone with a three-in-one game table.

OPPOSITE: A new queen-size bed with an upholstered headboard gives Michael, who is about 6 feet tall, the room he needs to stretch out. Tall, skinny bookcases do double duty as bedside tables and storage.

LEFT: This very cool storage and display system mounts on the wall with cleats. Metal dowels snap into the holes and support shelves, clips, and hooks. I chose a zebrawood finish to blend with the dark wood cabinetry.

STYLE ELEMENTS

- The canvas panel divider system consists of 4-foot-square panels that can be customized with printed graphics and then stretched onto tension poles. I chose a sophisticated black-and-white image of ice crystals for the lounge area side of the panels and a fun splatter pattern rub-on transfer for Michael's side.

- I gave the existing, boring sliding doors on the closet a major facelift with paint (see page 190–191). Squares of iridescent and pearlescent paints were applied, glazed, and then brushed for a strié finish, creating a high-style graphic effect.

- Fabrics for the whole space started with a contemporary floral. It only appears on a couple of accent pillows, but it's important because it's the key to the wall color—a pale gray-blue—and a taupey mushroomy teen-proof upholstery fabric for the two sofas.

- For Michael's bedroom, I upholstered a tufted headboard in a gray-blue microfiber to blend with the walls. Cocoa and espresso-brown bedding with taupe and black accents warm up the grays for a grown-up, masculine look.

- I hid the basement's single tiny window behind layered panels of incredible crushed velvet and patent leather. Rock on!

OPPOSITE: A macro-scaled image of ice crystals printed on a canvas panel is both temporary wall and artwork for the family room part of the basement. Big, comfy sofas covered in indestructible upholstery fabric are teen-proof for Michael's friends but stylish enough to keep Mom and Dad happy.

OPPOSITE: I masked the tiny window with layered draperies of crushed velvet that hang from ceiling to floor and create a cocoon-like effect at night.

BELOW: The big-screen TV is integrated into sleek, contemporary custom cabinetry that incorporates surround-sound speakers and includes storage for DVDs and video games. The same kind of component storage and display system that I installed in Michael's bedroom flanks the media center to show off art and photos.

OPPOSITE: A large closet with sliding doors now functions as a work of art, thanks to an easy paint treatment of pearlescent and iridescent squares with a strié finish. This end of the room is the games area with a three-in-one game table illuminated by a three-light chandelier.

OPPOSITE: A sleek new desk and chair give Michael a dedicated space to do his homework. The "antique" telephone and typewriter add a touch of humor!

LEFT: A beverage fridge built into the custom cabinet saves running upstairs for water or a soda. Michael's mom had requested a contemporary style for the design, and I was happy to oblige with this beautiful zebrawood furniture.

TWEEN-RIFIC AND MOM-APPROVED

CHALLENGE

"Tween-ager" Rachel was ready for a change in her very blue bedroom, with its little-girl piles of stuffed animals. The problem was that her tastes and her mother's were diametrically opposed. Rachel loves modern style, bold geometrics in pinks and oranges, and a look that says "fun." Mom Melanie prefers traditional style, with subtle florals in quiet neutrals, and she wants Rachel's room to work with the rest of the house. Both of them would like a functional fix for Rachel's piles of clutter. So it's Design Referee to the rescue, to come up with a plan that will please and appease them both.

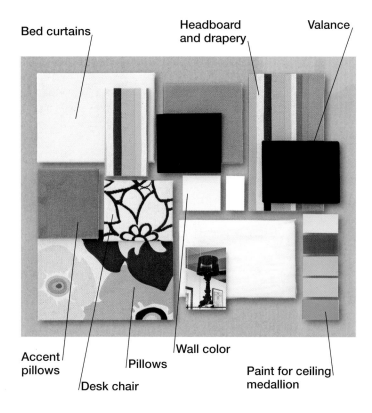

Bed curtains

Headboard and drapery

Valance

Accent pillows

Desk chair

Pillows

Wall color

Paint for ceiling medallion

BEFORE: Rachel was tired of her very blue walls, and her mother was tired of all the clutter. The desk was so piled with stuff that there was no space for doing homework.

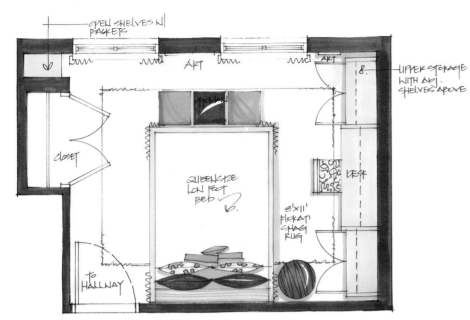

AFTER: A beautiful compromise: The envelope of neutral color and a wall of traditional-style cabinetry speak to Mom's concern that the room work with the rest of the house. Bold, well-placed splashes of pink, orange, and black express Rachel's creative personality and energy.

SOLUTION

- Kids come with 100 times their weight in stuff! The room didn't have nearly enough storage for all of Rachel's arts-and-crafts supplies, collections, and clothes, so everything ended up in piles all over the room. I remedied this situation right away with a whole wall of cabinetry—two units of closed storage flanking a desk and shelves. Rachel can use the shelves to showcase her artwork, and the desk meets Mom's requirement that Rachel at last have a place to do homework (sorry, Rachel!).

- I made the bed the room's focal point by designing a lavish, four-poster effect using yards of gauzy sheer fabric. The draperies hang by curtain clips from a ceiling-mounted metal rod so they can be pushed to the corners or drawn closed for a cocoon-like effect.

- The old ceiling fixture was not very tweeny, and I replaced it with a fun, twinkly fixture of crystal beads. To center the fixture over the bed, I needed to move it 10 inches, so I designed a totally fun and funky flower-shaped medallion to fasten to the ceiling and cover the old hole.

ABOVE: Striped draperies with deep black valances combine the colors that Rachel loves. You don't need a lot of strong color in a room to have a big impact—against a neutral background, bold, hot colors demand your attention and create an impression of more color than is actually there. Seating cubes covered in pink and black microfiber and pink and black accessories drive home the lively scheme.

STYLE ELEMENTS

- The real work of reconciling Rachel's and Melanie's contrasting tastes falls to the fabrics and finishes, and a high-contrast, high-energy, high-style scheme does the trick. The walls, the carpet, the bedding, and the cabinetry are all in quiet neutrals to satisfy Melanie and to provide longevity.

- To provide the punch of bold color that Rachel loves, I chose a striped fabric with her favorite hues—pink, orange, fuchsia, and black. The bright, modern stripe will have a big impact as floor-to-ceiling draperies on the room's two big windows, and it also slipcovers the headboard. Underneath the slipcover, the headboard is upholstered in a neutral that Melanie will like.

- Accent pillows in hot pink, black, and a bright 1970s-style floral really pop against the neutral bedding and increase the impression of color in the room. I also painted the ceiling medallion in colors taken from the fabrics.

- The cabinetry is very traditional in style but I gave it a shot of Rachel-pleasing fun with psychedelic pink acrylic panels. The panels attach to the cabinet's glass door panes with double-sided tape and can be easily removed. Lighting installed in the top of the cabinets makes the doors glow with luminescent color.

OPPOSITE: A chandelier of crystal beads hangs over the center of the bed for a decidedly grown-up, elegant touch. The ceiling medallion, on the other hand, falls on the side of fun and funky. Acrylic panels adhered to the inside of the cabinet's glass doors give a wacky psychedelic effect—and hide all the stuff inside!

BELOW: Ceiling medallions are my secret technique for avoiding having to patch holes when a fixture needs to be moved! Cut from wood and firmly nailed to the ceiling, this painted flower was inspired by one of the accent fabrics for the bed.

ABOVE: The pretty bed curtains can be drawn around the bed to create a cocoon-like feeling or pushed to the wall and corners for a four-poster effect.

BELOW: Melanie wanted Rachel to have a desk area for homework. An acrylic chair with an eye-popping black-and-white floral pattern might make studying more appealing to Rachel. The shelves above were designed as a gallery for rotating displays of her artwork.

GARDEN-FAIRY FANTASY

CHALLENGE

One-year-old Eliana and big sister Talia (age 4) are now old enough to share a room, so the attic guest room will become their new digs. It's a big space with good bones, but it has some problems—namely low, steeply angled ceilings and disproportionately low windows. Its biggest asset is a beautiful view out the window to an incredible magnolia tree and garden. Parents Tara and Scott don't want the room to be stereotypically feminine with lots of frilly pink and white. Rather, they want it to be a fun, creative place for the girls to play and develop their imaginations (and to sleep). And the best part is, I have their permission to go a little bit over the top!

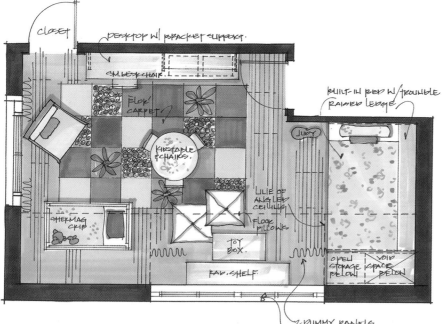

AFTER: Steep eaves and quirky angles are turned to advantage to create this attic aerie for little fairies. I painted each girl's name on the wall over her bed to define her space and established shared storage and play areas with the furniture arrangement. (Note the butterflies on the wall!)

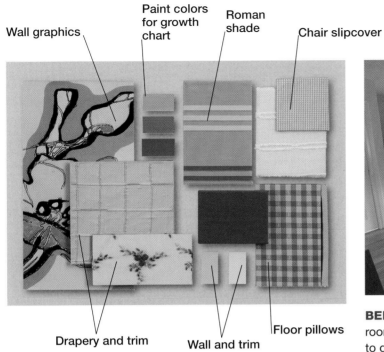

Wall graphics

Paint colors for growth chart

Roman shade

Chair slipcover

Drapery and trim

Wall and trim

Floor pillows

BEFORE: The attic was a catchall space and occasional guest room, but the steeply angled ceilings made it a real challenge to decorate. The windows were very low and out of scale with the room, and with a radiator right underneath, window treatments were a problem.

SOLUTION

- I summoned my inner child, looked at the magnolia tree, and got my inspiration: Eliana and Talia's room would become the home of a secret society of garden fairies!

- To give each little girl her own space, I designated one side of the room to be Talia's and one side to be Eliana's, and nestled each of their beds under the eaves. Eliana is still in a crib for now, but for Talia I designed a new platform bed with open storage shelves below and a pull-out trundle bed for fairy cousins who come to visit.

- Along the long wall I designed a shared space for creative activities, with a (very classy) wall-mounted tabletop, bookshelves, and bins for toys (see page 208–209). A toy chest on the opposite wall provides more shared storage.

- The room had little in the way of light fixtures, and there was no space in the attic for recessed fixtures, so I installed halogen track lighting to highlight the walls.

OPPOSITE: Talia's custom-built platform bed rests atop open storage and a trundle bed. A boxlike unit against the wall serves as a bedside table, and another at the end of the bed provides more storage space.

LEFT: Carpet tiles are a kid-rific way to warm up the hardwood floors. Mix and match them to compose a larger carpet, then remove the sticky tabs on the back and press them into place.

STYLE ELEMENTS

- The walls in the attic were a blank canvas for my wacky ideas, and I made the most of them! I found the most incredible handmade wallpaper mural of fantasy flowers and used it as the starting point for a whole roomful of hand-painted butterflies and cartoon flowers sprouting everywhere. I also had Talia's and Eliana's names painted over their respective beds and a flowery growth chart painted on the activity center wall.

- To disguise the awkward proportions of the windows, I designed a Roman shade that extends up onto the ceiling, creating the illusion of a continuous window. Dummy panels made from a box-stitched polished cotton edged with a gorgeous, very feminine rosette lace frame the view to the garden. A little scalloped valance between the panels suggests a garden canopy over the window. Bridging the fantasy world with the practical one, the Roman shades are lined with blackout lining to darken the room for naps.

- The hardwood floors were beautiful, so I simply created a kid-friendly carpeted area in the center of the room with carpet tiles. These super-cool tiles come in a multitude of colors and patterns and can be assembled into a larger carpet. The tiles adhere with sticky tabs that won't damage hardwood floors. When accidents happen, the individual tiles can be pulled up and cleaned or replaced.

- I pulled colors from the mural and came up with a scheme that's fun and feminine but not too precious—very pale green for the walls and soft apple greens, bright pinks, and light creams for the fabrics.

- Under the side window, I placed a chair for reading bedtime stories and a glass pendant chandelier that looks like crystal (this is about fantasy, after all!).

LEFT: The striped fabric of the Roman shades continues up the wall to create the illusion of an extended window. The drapery panels, edged with a beautiful rosette-studded lace, are threaded onto partial rods to frame the view. I tied them back at the level of the windowsill to create a longer, more graceful line.

OPPOSITE: The window treatments are all about tricking the eye into perceiving the low windows as much higher than they really are. A "crystal" (okay, it's glass) chandelier hangs above a simple slipcovered chair for reading before bedtime.

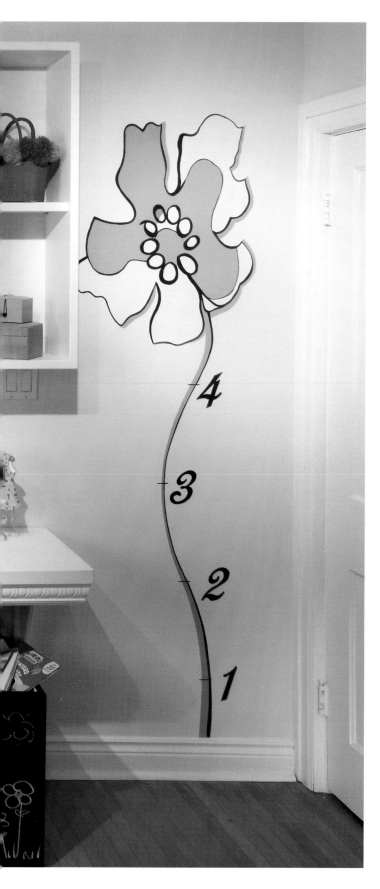

ABOVE: Good fairies always pick up their toys. It's easier with simple MDF (medium-density fiberboard) boxes. Painted with blackboard paint, they're perfect surfaces for creative self-expression in chalk.

OPPOSITE: The fabulous hand-painted wallpaper mural inspired the color scheme as well as hand-painted graphics around the room. This handsome wall-mounted counter gives the girls a place to draw and paint now and can become a desk for homework when they're older.

TODDLER TERRIFIC

CHALLENGE

New parents Tatiana and Mario thought they had plenty of time to prepare a nursery for the baby they were planning to adopt. Then word came that Adriana was on her way—in three weeks! Plans for decorating a nursery were shelved as they dove into parenthood. Now that a few years have gone by, they're ready to turn Mario's cluttered home office into Adriana's room and they need some help.

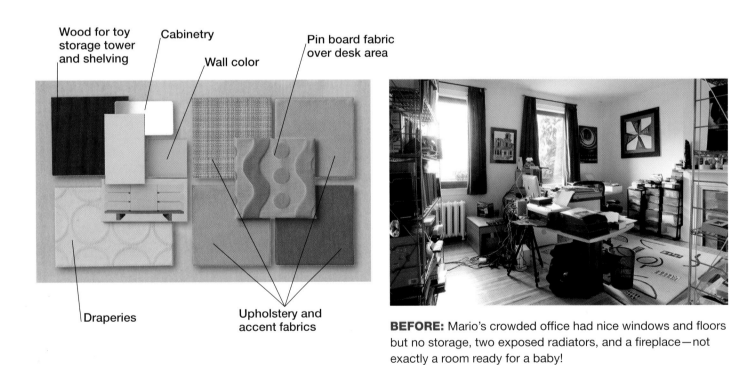

Wood for toy storage tower and shelving

Cabinetry

Wall color

Pin board fabric over desk area

Draperies

Upholstery and accent fabrics

BEFORE: Mario's crowded office had nice windows and floors but no storage, two exposed radiators, and a fireplace—not exactly a room ready for a baby!

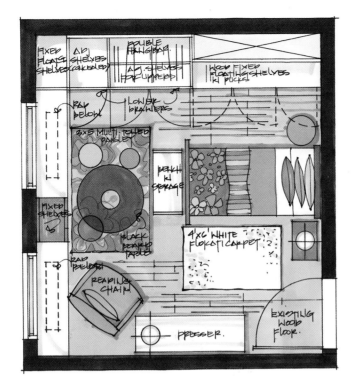

AFTER: New closets, drawers, and shelves supply loads of storage for Adriana's clothes and toys. A menagerie of stuffed animals peeks out from portholes in the custom-built storage tower. Narrow shelves tucked into the sliver of space in the corner provide more places to stash stuff and keep things organized. The custom-built white cabinets are a blank canvas for whimsical contemporary peel-and-stick graphics in fun kid colors.

SOLUTION

- Underneath all the stacks of papers, books, and office clutter I discovered a lovely room with big windows, hardwood floors, a fireplace, and absolutely no storage. The fireplace was not appropriate for a child's room so I moved the mantel into storage, stuffed the opening full of insulation, and sealed it up.

- I designed an entire bank of floor-to-ceiling cabinetry that extends from the fireplace all the way to the window wall. Upper cabinets hold hanging clothes, and drawers below hold toys for now and shoes later.

- I covered the fireplace area with drywall and installed shelves and a desk with more storage below. Adriana can use this area for arts and crafts now and homework later. Colorful "mushroom" stools will boost her and her friends high enough for coloring on the work surface.

- I encased the radiators in boxes with grills to allow for hot-air circulation.

- Sandwiched between the windows is a floor-to-ceiling, custom-built storage tower with open access along the side and through fun porthole openings in the front.

- Adriana has nearly outgrown her crib, so I brought in a "big girl" twin bed that's low enough for a little one to crawl into.

OPPOSITE: Sleek cabinetry gives the room the contemporary "architecture" Tatiana wanted, and the storage and display areas will work as well for Adriana when she's a teen as they do for her now. Puck lights installed under each shelf wash light down onto the surface below and illuminate the desk for play.

OPPOSITE: A fabric-covered push-pin board puts pattern and color on the wall above the desk, and mirror-backed shelves add depth and light. To draw and color at the desk, Adriana can climb up on her choice of colorful mushroom stools.

BELOW: The best thing about a no-color design is adding color, and bed linens, pillows, and artwork all bring in lots of exciting color to spark Adriana's imagination and creativity.

ABOVE: These little orange lounge chairs are just too cute for words! With an oh-so-cool white shag rug, Adriana's "seating area" is the epitome of chic modern style.

STYLE ELEMENTS

- Tatiana and Mario had renovated the rest of their early 1900s home in a very contemporary style, so I brought that same sensibility into Adriana's room. The custom cabinetry has contemporary flat-front doors and drawer faces, with sleek metal bars for drawer and door pulls. A dresser on the opposite wall is also ultra-contemporary.

- I contrasted the white-painted cabinetry and radiator boxes with dark-stained wood that picks up on the wood of the window frames. The floating shelves, desk, storage tower, and top of the radiator boxes all wear a warm brown stain, creating a clean, graphic contrast with the white cabinetry.

- To make this room flexible enough to grow with Adriana, I painted the walls an easy-to-live-with near-white. Happy, festive color comes in by way of bed linens, accessories, and fabric on the wall behind the desk. For a touch of whimsy, I decorated the cabinet doors and windows with peel-and-stick graphics. They're fun, funky, and easy to remove when Adriana outgrows them.

- I dressed the windows simply, with grommet-top panels stitched from a cream-color microfiber with a subtle but modern pattern of interlocking circles. I hung them near the ceiling to stretch the apparent height of the windows and hemmed them to fall just above the top of the radiator boxes.

- The lighting plan is designed for longevity, too. There was no room overhead for recessed lights, so I installed halogen track lighting around the perimeter of the room to spotlight the cabinets and storage tower. Each window is accented with a sparkly little pendant fixture. As a crowning touch of whimsy, a chandelier that looks like a mobile with little halogen-lit crystal drops dangles over the bed.

LEFT: The peel-and-stick graphics continue onto the window, where a miniature crystal-cube pendant light twinkles by day and sparkles at night. Creamy microfiber curtains are easy to clean and great for kids' rooms.

This contemporary dresser has the kind of longevity Tatiana wanted for the room. Mom or Dad can sit in the modern side chair now, but it will serve Adriana's needs as she grows. Flower-power pillows around the room add color and lighthearted style.

INDEX

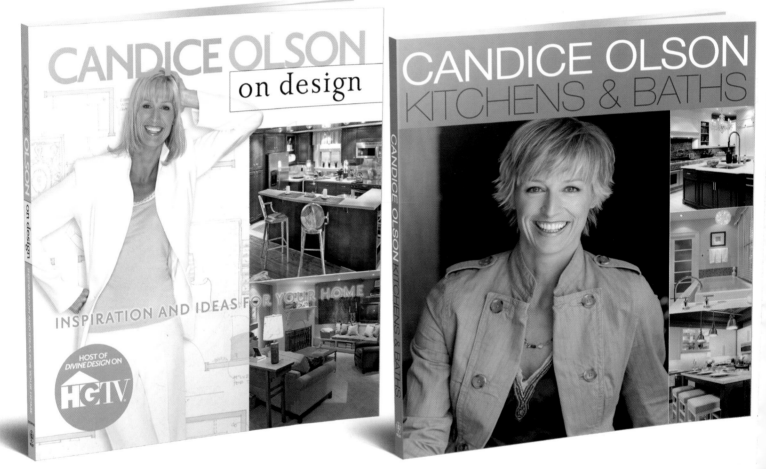
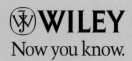